China: Tradition and Revolution

PETER M. MITCHELL
Department of History
York University

Study material prepared by
DOUGLAS M. PARKER
Head of History
Thistletown Collegiate Institute
Rexdale, Ontario

EDWARD ARNOLD

ISBN: 0 7131 0110 5

Sources of quotations: pages 228-31

Sources of illustrations: Jerome Ch'en, York University: p. 119; *China Pictorial*: pp. 2 (upper left, lower), 11, 15 (right); Field Museum of Natural History, Chicago: p. 47; M. Gewurtz, York University: p. 51; Patricia Kennedy: pp. 2 (upper right), 112; Miller Services Ltd.: pp. 8, 9 (lower, Richard Harrington), 40 (lower, Richard Harrington), 63 (lower, Richard Harrington), 143, 166, 170, 192 (Richard Harrington), 193, 199 (upper, Richard Harrington), 209, 213, 215; P. M. Mitchell and M. Quealey: pp. 15 (left), 16, 18, 66, 174, 186, 200; Radio Times Hulton Picture Library: pp. 100 (upper), 122; Smithsonian Institution, Freer Gallery of Art, Washington, D.C.: p. 100 (lower).

Cover photos courtesy of Miller Services Ltd.

Maps by James Loates

Printed in Canada

PREFACE

This small volume is not a detailed outline of Chinese history; it is, rather, an analytic account of the major historical developments that have gone into the shaping of contemporary China. The approach is generally sympathetic—perhaps too much so for those who condemn China as an atheistic, violent, and undemocratic society. But the real aim of this study is understanding, and it is my belief that understanding can come only through approaching contemporary China in terms of China's own past; then, if one wishes, comparisons can be made with other underdeveloped countries. Finally, and only with great caution, comparisons can be made with our own society. With this approach we can hope to avoid either a quick negative reaction to China, resulting in the closing of our minds to her unique qualities and achievements, or an equally quick positive reaction, such as has sometimes been accompanied by a simplistic enthusiasm for borrowing from the Chinese experience.

Today, one-quarter of the world's population lives in the People's Republic of China. Surely that demands from us a measure of real understanding.

A note about names and dates: Names of people are given as in Chinese—that is, with the surname first and the personal name following; for example, Mao Tse-tung is Chairman Mao, Tse-tung being his personal name. All names, including place names, are written in the standard transliteration, except where popular usage has made alternative spellings more common. The Pronunciation Guide (see page 226) will aid readers not used to Chinese pronunciations.

Dates are referred to as B.C.E. (Before Common Era) and C.E. (Common Era). These terms correspond exactly to B.C. and A.D., but are preferred because the latter have no meaning in Chinese history.

PETER M. MITCHELL

CONTENTS

LIST OF MAPS

SECTION I
THE TRADITIONAL
BACKGROUND

Contrasts: south China coastline (upper l.); southwest mountain range, with old city wall and gate (upper r.); Gobi Desert in northwest (lower).

CHAPTER 1
The Environment

China is a land of striking geographic diversity. The third-largest country in the world after Russia and Canada, it contains within its borders tropical jungles and arid desert wastes, flatlands below sea level and mountain peaks. Green rice paddies, hillside terraces of tea plants, waving prairies of golden wheat, sparse garden-size plots carved out of rocky hillsides — all these reflect a wide variety of cultivation skills, evolved through centuries of Chinese ingenuity. To understand any country requires an acquaintance with its geography, but it is equally important to know how people have related and responded to the land on which they live. In this chapter we will examine briefly the historical interaction between the Chinese land and its people.

Compare the topographical and population-density maps (Maps 1 and 2). Three large river valleys support the highest density of population. In the north, the turbulent Yellow River flows from Tibet to the Pacific Ocean. In central China, the Yangtze covers a distance of more than 51 000 kilometres and forms, in its lower reaches, a flat delta, crisscrossed by elaborate secondary networks of canals and smaller streams. In the southeast, the West River or Sikiang (sometimes also called the Pearl River) is less extensive than the two more northern river systems, but forms an important delta region around the city of Canton. Through history, these three rivers and their surrounding

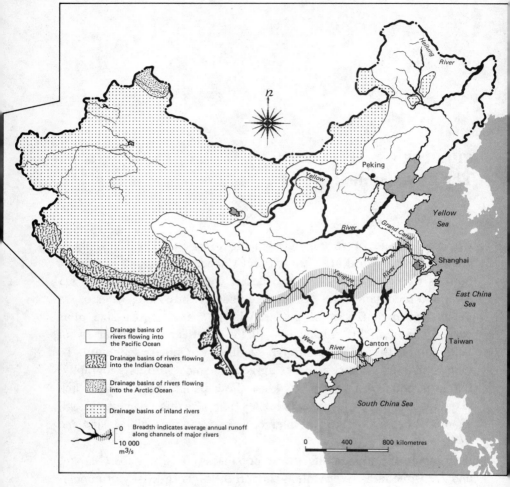

Map 1A   China's Topography: Major Rivers

valleys provided the main environmental influences on China's way of life.

Distinctive climates mark the three great river valleys. In the north, hot, dry summers alternate with cold winters. In contrast, the West River (or Canton) delta enjoys a warm, moist, semitropical climate.

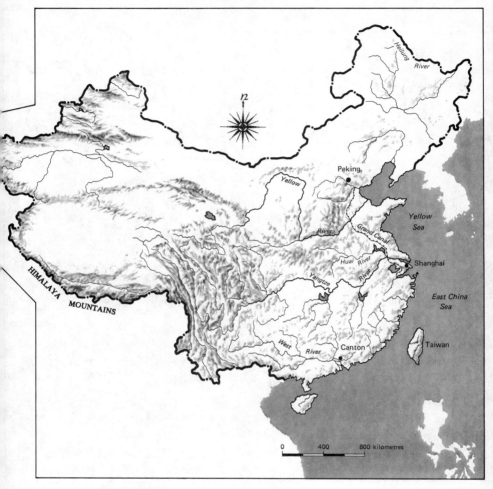

Map 1B   China's Topography: Mountains

Winters are short and mild, summers hot and humid. Rainfall is abundant, and sometimes overabundant when, eight or nine times each year, typhoons sweep in from the South Pacific during the late summer. In between these two extremes, the Yangtze basin has a more moderate climate. Hills north of the river protect against the worst of

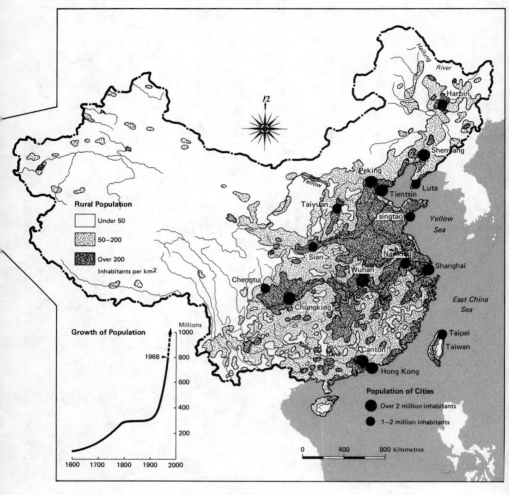

Map 2   Density and Growth of Population (1968)

the winter's cold, while those to the south blunt the force of the typhoons. Summer is generally long, warm, and pleasantly moist; winters are short and mild. This climatic diversity had a profound effect on China's cultural development.

Crops and methods of farming in each of these regions reflect most strikingly the geographic and climatic variations (see Map 3). In the

Yellow River region, moisture is scarce and very unpredictable. Drought is a constant problem; and yet the same area can suffer from disastrous floods, resulting from either sudden torrential downpours or the overflow of the Yellow River, also called "China's Sorrow."

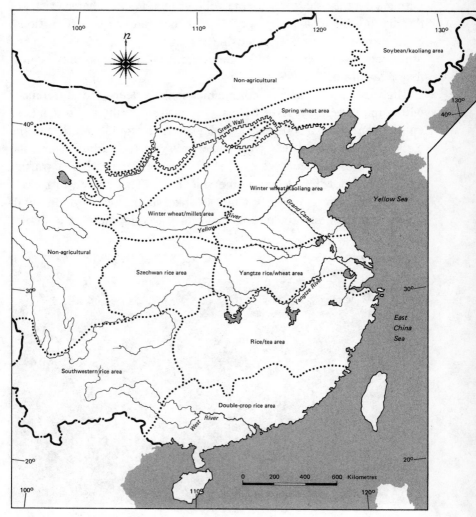

Map 3   Agricultural Regions

Dry-land crops predominate, and farming techniques are geared toward preserving scarce moisture. In the southeast regions around the West River delta, the distinctive crop is rice, which is grown in small, flooded paddy fields that often ascend in regular steps up the hillsides. Semitropical fruits, palm trees, bamboo groves, and hillsides covered with tea contrast sharply with the yellows and browns characteristic of the dry north-China landscape. Again, the Yangtze is a transitional area, growing crops and practising the farming methods of both the other regions. Adaptability to environmental variations has been a major feature of China's long history.

The nature of internal communications reflects the differences within the three great river basins. The historic birthplace of Chinese civilization, some 3 500 years ago, lay along the middle reaches of the Yellow River. Since this great waterway was too turbulent and the adjoining coastal waters were too shallow to sustain much boat traffic, the Chinese developed land communications. This helped to form a uniform culture as the early Chinese state spread outward. In south China, the hills and rivers prevented easy development of a similar

The Yangtze, with the road-and-rail bridge built in 1957 at Wuhan.

The Pearl River at Canton, with a traditional sampan (upper); the Yellow River, with new dikes protecting the flat north China plain (lower).

complex of roads, and cultural uniformity took longer to achieve and was less complete. As Chinese people and civilization moved southward, the carts and wheelbarrows of the north were replaced by sampans and junks as the major mode of transport in the easily navigable coastal waters and inland rivers. Numerous canals were built, particularly in the lower Yangtze delta. The most famous example of this ancient Chinese art was the Grand Canal, first completed in the early seventh century to connect the agricultural wealth of the Yangtze basin with the traditional centre of political power in the northern plain.

Major linguistic divisions broadly reflected geographic features. Mandarin, or Peking-based, dialects were typical of the northern areas; along the Yangtze there were several others, for example the Wu dialect near the coast and the Szechwan dialect in its upper reaches. Cantonese was the most common of several dialects in the southeast. These linguistic variations posed great problems, not only to the westerner trying to learn Chinese, but also to Chinese rulers who sought to unify the entire country. The major difficulty arose because the dialects are orally distinct, even though the written language is the same throughout. Moreover, until the recent spread of mass education, literacy was limited to the very few.

Thus far, we have confined our discussion to only a small part of China. The reason is simple. It is within these areas primarily that Chinese culture developed. (See Map 2.) Until modern times, the cold inhospitality of the far northern regions held little attraction for the Chinese. To the west, the deserts, mountains, and semi-arid plains could not sustain large agricultural settlements. The extreme southwest was either too hilly or too high in altitude for much intensive agriculture. People did (and do) live in these vast regions; a high proportion of them belonged to ''national minority'' groups or, in North American terms, ethnic communities. In these areas, the main Chinese cultural element (called the Han people) constituted only a small percentage of mainly administrative personnel. Today such minority peoples represent about ten per cent of China's total population.

Geographic barriers on all sides enabled China to nurture its own distinctive culture in relative isolation from potential rivals. Beginning

Northwest, showing women of a non-Chinese ethnic group.

Northwest grazing lands, showing flocks and a tent (yurt) of the nomadic people.

thousands of years ago, the Chinese developed, in the Yellow River valley, a culture that gradually forced out or incorporated all rival cultures within that region. Other peoples were compelled to surrender to assimilation or to migrate outward to the less desirable fringes of the expanding Chinese cultural zone. As the Chinese moved gradually southward, the hills and other physical barriers below the Yangtze allowed pockets of such peoples to resist full assimilation. Still, from the arid wastes of Mongolia's Gobi Desert and Siberia's frozen tundra right down to the barrier of tropical jungle and Himalayan Mountains separating southwest China from India (the other major early Asian civilization), the Chinese found no other advanced culture. The Chinese thus came to view all surrounding cultures as inferior or outright barbaric.

Throughout China's history, the physical environment has challenged its people. Regional diversities at times hampered political efforts for greater national unity, while at other times those same diversities helped preserve Chinese civilization when major portions of the north fell under alien conquerors. To the frustration of successive governments (but to the enrichment of Chinese folklore and literature), the isolated, hilly regions within the country also provided sanctuary for various dissident groups. These included hermits, bandit gangs, and rebel bands. The most famous modern example of such reliance on the natural environment is the Chinese Communist Party. Frequently, during its struggles against the Nationalist government and the Japanese invaders, during the 1930s and 1940s, the Party relied on natural sanctuaries for protection.

Analysis

1. Why would a country of vast size and diverse geographic regions be more difficult to govern than a small, relatively uniform area?

2. In what ways are your own country and China similar or different in this regard?

3. What government policies would you suggest in order to overcome such geographical problems?

4. Consider the advantages and disadvantages of geographical diversity. What are the advantages and disadvantages as they relate to China?

Suggested Readings

(*Note:* In this and other Suggested Readings throughout the text, the titles are available in paperback unless otherwise indicated.)

George Cressey, *Land of the 500 Million: A Geography of China* (New York: McGraw-Hill, 1955). (Hardcover)

Standard reference with excellent maps and illustrations.

Geography of China (Peking: Foreign Language Press, 1972).

Useful pamphlet-length treatment for general use.

T. R. Tregear, *A Geography of China* (Chicago: Aldine, 1965).

Good maps and more recent than Cressey, but less comprehensive. (Hardcover)

Tuan Yi-fu, *China*. The World's Landscapes, vol. 1 (London: Longman, 1970).

Excellent, short historical treatment, stressing interaction of Chinese social development and the geographical environment, complete with good maps, diagrams, and pictures.

CHAPTER 2
Traditional Social and Economic Patterns

A system of sedentary village agriculture, first developed in the north, formed the basis of Chinese civilization. From the second millennium B.C.E. to the middle of the twentieth century, the peasant farmer of China lived in a small village and followed a basically unchanging pattern of life. This economic system marked the great separation between the Chinese cultural unit and other, rival cultures in that part of Asia. The Chinese system of agriculture and village life permitted the Chinese to outstrip all neighbouring peoples in population, wealth, and cultural sophistication.

The peasant farmer of China was part of a small family unit of five or six members. The average holding for a peasant owner/cultivator was only one hectare in south China and perhaps four times that size in the less productive areas of north China. A "farm" usually consisted of a variety of small, scattered plots. Intensive methods of farming permitted a high level of production despite the small average size. In a description applicable to almost any period of Chinese history, two American journalists, Theodore H. White and Annalee Jacoby, depicted the nature of cultivation in central China in the 1940s:

> Men and women come together in the villages to produce children, till the land, and raise crops. The unity of man, village, and field is total and rigid. All the work is done by hand, from the sowing of the rice grains in early

spring, through the laborious transplanting of the tufts in water-filled paddies in late spring, to the final harvesting by sickle in the fall. The Chinese farmer does not farm; he gardens. He, his wife, and his children pluck out the weeds one by one. He hoards his family's night soil [human excrement] through all the months of the year; in the spring he ladles out of mortar pits huge stinking buckets of dark green liquid offal, and carefully, without wasting a drop, he spreads the life-giving nitrogen among his vegetables and plants. When harvest time comes, the whole family goes out to the field to bring in the grain. The family helps him thresh his grain, either by monotonously beating it with a flail or by guiding animals that draw huge stone rollers round and round in a circle over the threshing floor. All life is attached to the soil; the peasant works at it, eats of it, returns to it all that his body excretes, and is finally himself returned to the soil.

. . . Frugality governs all his actions. He gathers every wisp of grass and twists it together for fuel. He sows beans or vegetables on the narrow ridges that separate one paddy field from another, so that no square foot of growing land is lost. He weaves hats, baskets, and sandals out of rice straw; out of the pig's bladder he makes a toy balloon for the children; every piece of string, every scrap of paper, every rag is saved.[1]

Romanticized by some writers, bluntly labelled as brutal by others, this was the life-style over the centuries for the massive majority of China's population.

Traditional agricultural methods, still seen today: rice-paddy cultivation by water-buffalo and mattock (left); weeding of fields by mass collective labour (right).

More traditional agricultural methods still practised: threshing by hand in north China (upper); irrigation by foot-powered water ladder feeding pond water to neighbouring rice paddies (lower).

With a mere twelve per cent of China's total land area suitable for this type of agriculture, food was precious and often scarce. Grains and vegetables constituted ninety per cent of average meals, and protein foods were used more as a garnish than as bulk. Protein came primarily from soy-bean derivatives in the north and from fish and other marine products in the south. To a lesser extent, pork and chicken were included, particularly in the diet of those who were well off. Sheep and goats were found mainly on the grasslands of the northwest, and dairy products were known only among non-Chinese border peoples. With limited land resources and a high population, the Chinese could not afford the luxury of raising herds of animals for food. Large animals were restricted to draught purposes — the water-buffalo in the south and the ox and donkey in the north. The succulent menu offerings of North American Chinese restaurants were known only to the richest families; such delights were totally beyond the means of the peasant.

The peasant's lot was a hard one. While he might dream of economic self-sufficiency and independence, he had to co-ordinate the planting, irrigation, and harvesting of his scattered fields with those of his neighbours. Furthermore, his village had to stand as a co-operative unit in relation to neighbouring villages sharing the same water source. If a peasant owned his own land, money taxes required that he market his crop to obtain the coin demanded by the tax collector. Also, labour taxes forced the peasant to co-operate with his neighbours to maintain local government-sponsored public works such as roads, canals, and irrigation systems. The society's traditions required that he expend substantial cash on such occasions as the burial of a parent or the marriage of a daughter. These political and social obligations frequently forced the peasant into borrowing. Loans were secured against possessions, and high interest rates made repayment very difficult. Although society put a high premium on a man's legacy to his descendants, observers have noted that the average peasant's only bequest was a crippling load of unpaid debts. Thus the ideals of self-sufficiency, security, and independence were only rarely achieved by a peasant household.

Whenever natural disasters, such as a flood, a drought, or a plague of insects, combined with the heavy burden of taxes and high interest rates on loans, the peasant was easily pushed below his slim margin of subsistance. In such circumstances, a peasant could lose his land and become a tenant or a labourer; and peasant households in these categories always represented a sizeable minority in most Chinese

Intensive agriculture: barren hills in south China, stripped in the past for fuel and forage, now gradually being reforested (upper); tiny fields carved out of a rocky hillside in north China (lower).

villages. In even worse times, when famine threatened the whole community, the result might be the premature death of the older members of the family, the sale of young daughters to some rich household, or even the breaking up of family units. Famines were a periodic fact of life well into the present century. An official report to the emperor in the early seventeenth century depicts the nature of famine conditions in the north:

> Yenan, the prefecture from which your humble servant comes, has not had any rain for more than a year. Trees and grass are all dried up. During the eighth and ninth months of last year people went to the mountains to collect raspberries which were called grain but actually were no better than chaff. They tasted bitter and could only postpone death for the time being. By the tenth month all the raspberries were gone, and the people peeled off tree bark as food. . . . Towards the end of the year the supply of tree bark was exhausted, and they had to go to the mountains to dig up stones for food. Stones were cold and tasted musty. A little taken in would fill up the stomach. Those who took stones found their stomachs swollen and they dropped and died in a few days. Others who had no wish to eat stones gathered as bandits. They robbed the few who had some savings, and when they robbed, they took everything and left nothing behind. Their idea was that since they had to die either one way or another it was preferable to die as a bandit than to die from hunger and that to die as a bandit would enable them to enter the next world with a full stomach. . . .[2]

The report continued, describing the abandonment of infants, the presence of cannibalism, and the sight and smell of hundreds of unburied corpses.

A surprisingly similar tale, again by the American newspaper correspondent Theodore H. White, describes a famine in Honan province in 1942:

> The strong had fled earlier; all who were left now were the old, the weak, and the few hardy characters who were staying to guard the spring wheat that would soon be in full growth. The people were slicing bark from elm trees, grinding it to eat as food. Some were tearing up the roots of the new wheat; in other villages people were living on pounded peanut husks or refuse. Refugees on the road had been seen madly cramming soil into their mouths to fill their bellies, and the missionary hospitals were stuffed with people suffering from terrible intestinal obstructions due to the filth they were eating.[3]

This modern report goes on to describe similar looting, abandonment of children, and cannibalism.

In the past, in the final desperate stages of such conditions, masses of peasants rose in rebellion and frequently toppled the existing political regime. A new administrative order would result, but such changes never fundamentally altered the basic life-style of the peasant majority.

Despite the predominance of agriculture, China's economy and social structure did change throughout the centuries of its traditional history. Changes lacked spectacular abruptness, but they were nevertheless significant. For example, from the eleventh century onward, the spread of rice cultivation and the increasing importance of two other southern crops—tea and cotton—resulted in a distinct shift of the Chinese centre of both population and wealth southward to the Yangtze. The rich productivity of the more southern areas produced sufficient new wealth to sustain a much more complex social structure. As commercial cities grew up, a bustling domestic and foreign trade developed. Cheaper water transportation allowed various regions to specialize in certain crops most suitable for their soil and climate, counting on more distant markets for sale of their produce. The great wealth of China impressed and surprised Marco Polo, the thirteenth-century Venetian adventurer:

> To sum up, I can tell you in all truthfulness that the business of the province of Manzi [in central China] — its riches, its revenue and the profit derived from it by the Great Khan—is on such a stupendous scale that no one who hears tell of it without seeing it for himself can possibly credit it. Indeed it is scarcely possible to set down in writing the magnificence of this province.[4]

His doubts were well founded; his enthusiastic descriptions were indeed too startling for his European contemporaries to believe.

During the sixteenth and seventeenth centuries, new forms of agricultural productivity again set in motion fundamental social changes that took centuries to mature. New crops introduced from abroad, such as maize, sweet potatoes, and peanuts, allowed greater yields from marginal soil. This increased productivity permitted further urbanization and commercialization, still without altering the basic pattern of the agrarian society. Most important, it permitted a dramatic growth in population that has continued until this day. Estimates indicate that there were 150 million Chinese in the late sixteenth century, about 300 million in the late eighteenth century, 400 million by 1900, and at present about 800 million, representing one-quarter of the world's population. In the early stages of this upward spiral, increased productivity from available acreage sustained the growth pattern. When, in roughly the late eighteenth century, the numbers of people started to outstrip the economy's capacity, the precarious equation of life *versus* food supply emerged as an ominous backdrop to much of China's modern history.

The Chinese peasant represented consistently eighty to eighty-five per cent of the total population, and ultimately, the remaining members of the society depended upon the peasant class. The cultural élite, though making up a small minority, always drew a substantial portion of its income from landownership. This élite did not participate in productive enterprises; its superior position depended on its control of government and its domination of society. Members of the élite class were distinguished from the common people by their emphasis on intellectual activity. Many social practices developed around that difference. Three examples will suffice. The long, scholar's gown of the élite male contrasted with the 2 000-year-old peasant costume of trousers for both male and female. In both sexes, long fingernails were another mark of privilege, a visual sign of freedom from any form of physical labour. And finally, there were the "lily-feet" which distinguished upper-class women from others. This custom appeared with the growth of urban centres in south China from the twelfth century onward. When she was young, a girl's feet would be bound so tightly in cloth wrappings that their natural growth was impeded and they remained only about half their normal size. People viewed such abnormalities as physical attractions, and the virtual crippling of females became a status symbol for the men who could thus afford to incapacitate the womenfolk of their families. Lower-class families copied this practice for their attractive daughters, hoping that it would help their chances for acceptance as wives or concubines in wealthier households.

In the social hierarchy, at least in theory, the peasant stood just below the élite; below the peasants stood the artisans and then the merchants. This reflected the imagined basic alliance between the essential producers, the peasants, and the essential brains, the élite. Artisans were considered producers, but as their products were primarily luxury goods, they ranked lower in status than peasants. Merchants were ranked last as totally unproductive parasites, neither producing anything nor using their minds for anything other than pursuit of profit. In practice, however, the masses of peasants were very poor, while artisans and merchants frequently lived in considerable luxury. Nevertheless, the latter never successfully challenged the traditional hierarchy. A wealthy artisan or merchant family achieved social success only by acquiring sufficient capital to invest in land and educate its sons, thus escaping the stigma of the commercial classes by entry into the élite.

Analysis

1. Discuss the advantages and disadvantages of the village life pursued for thousands of years in China.

2. Compare the patterns described in this chapter with those of the feudal states in Europe during the Middle Ages.

3. Why would an overwhelmingly agricultural society have a cultural élite such as the one China had?

4. How is the ranking of various groups brought about in a society? What does the ranking reveal in Chinese society?

5. How does an élite perpetuate itself? How did the élite in China perpetuate itself?

Suggested Readings

J. L. Buck, "Chinese Agriculture," in A. Feuerwerker, ed., *Modern China* (Englewood Cliffs, N.J.: Prentice-Hall, 1964), 41–56.

   A short, general overview, drawn from his detailed *Land Utilization in China* (Nanking, 1937), representing the results of the most detailed field study of Chinese agriculture in the early twentieth century.

P. Buck, *The Good Earth* (New York: John Day, 1931).

   A romanticized but highly moving novel based on the peasant's life-style and problems; it is still useful to impart a general knowledge of peasant conditions and attitudes.

J. M. Gibson and D. M. Johnston, eds., *A Century of Struggle: Canadian Essays on Revolutionary China* (Toronto: Canadian Institute of International Relations, 1971).

Two chapters in particular: P. Mitchell, "The Peasant in Pre-revolutionary China," and J. Salaff, "The Family, Past and Present," provide useful short readings for high-school students.

R. Latham, *The Travels of Marco Polo* (London: Penguin Books, 1958).

One of many works on Marco Polo, this book presents his journals in readable style.

CHAPTER 3
The Politics of Imperial China

Chronology

1766?–1122 (1027?) B.C.E.	Shang dynasty
1122 (1027)–221 B.C.E.	Chou dynasty
221–206 B.C.E.	Ch'in dynasty
206 B.C.E.–220 C.E.	Han dynasty
220–589	First Period of Disunity
589–618	Sui dynasty
618–906	T'ang dynasty
906–960	Second Period of Disunity
960–1279	Sung dynasty
1279–1368	Yüan (Mongol) dynasty
1368–1644	Ming dynasty
1644–1911	Ch'ing (Manchu) dynasty

Chinese historians of traditional times usually conceived of time in terms of political divisions called "dynasties", that is, periods ranging from a few years to several centuries during which the throne of China was occupied by a single royal family. Thus, instead of a date such as 1840 being used, in Chinese terms the events of that year occurred in the twentieth year of the reign of the Tao-kuang emperor of the Ch'ing dynasty. Readers would know that that emperor's reign began in what westerners call 1820, and that the Ch'ing dynasty stretched back to what we call 1644. Here, we shall refer to dynasties by name, but we shall add the western dates. The accompanying chronological chart will serve as reference for our discussion which will focus on only two themes: first, the theory of legitimate political power, and second, the nature of the traditional political structure.

Political Thought

Present-day archaeology is constantly probing further back in the mists of time that cover the origins of Chinese civilization. The oldest authenticated political entity in China was a loose federation of "city-states" that lay within the middle Yellow River valley. This was the Shang dynasty, named after the chief city. Its rulers based their political claims primarily on divine authority and superior cultural attainments. The Shang were overthrown in the twelfth century B.C.E. by the Chou people, who justified their violent seizure of power partially in religious terms. They claimed that Heaven (*T'ien*), in its dissatisfaction with the corrupt tyranny of the last Shang rulers, had designated the Chou as legitimate successors. Thus, Heaven's Mandate (*T'ien-ming*) to rule was interpreted as transferable when an incumbent line failed to meet standards of good government.

Under Chou rule, conquest and a growing population vastly increased the size of the political unit. (See Map 4a, p. 26.) Unable to rule directly all parts of this expanded "China," the Chou developed a highly structured feudal-state system. The Chou king conferred titles and lands on aristocratic lords who governed their own regions. Theoretically, at least, these feudal strongmen were not independent heads of state; rather they were nobles, ranked within an aristocratic hierarchy. The Chou royal family stood at the apex of this hierarchy. As the Shang had done, the Chou court cultivated cultural superiority to reinforce their divine claims. The splendour and deliberate order of their urban capital were created to invoke a sense of awe, and hence a willingness to accept their authority. With the same end in mind, in this city's palaces and temples they developed elaborate court rituals and detailed codes of gentlemanly behaviour.

Although military force undoubtedly formed a basic ingredient of political power, it was cloaked with a screen of religious and cultural claims; political effectiveness depended to some extent upon people's

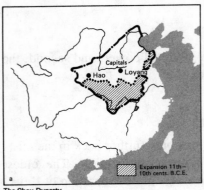

Capitals
● Hao ● Loyang

Expansion 11th–
10th cents. B.C.E.

a

The Chou Dynasty

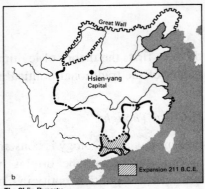

Great Wall

● Hsien-yang
Capital

Expansion 211 B.C.E.

b

The Ch'in Dynasty

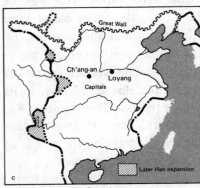

Great Wall

● Ch'ang-an
● Loyang
Capitals

Later Han expansion

c

The Earlier and Later Han Dynasties

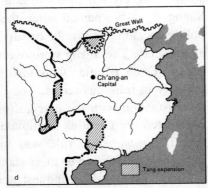

Great Wall

● Ch'ang-an
Capital

Tang expansion

d

The Sui and Tang Dynasties

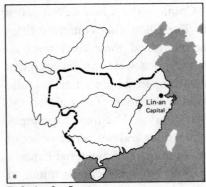

● Lin-an
Capital

e

The Southern Sung Dynasty

Great Wall

● Peking
Capitals

Grand Canal

Yingtien (Nanking) ●

1407–28

f

The Ming Dynasty

Map 4

Historical Maps (Capitals: a, Hao before 770 B.C.E., Loyang 770–221 B.C.E.; c, Ch'ang-an 206 B.C.E.–25 C.E., Loyang 25–220 C.E.; f, Nanking 1368–1421, Peking 1421–1644.)

willingness to accept such claims as legitimate. But as the Chou period wore on and the outlying feudal states developed in population and wealth, their lords paid less heed to the central court's pretensions. From the fifth century B.C.E. onward, the peripheral states ignored the capital's authority and began a process of absorbing the less powerful states around them. Sheer strength became the chief criterion of political legitimacy. After years of fighting, one state emerged supreme over all the others. In 221 B.C.E., by the fact of military power rather than any claims of divine or cultural superiority, the Ch'in became the new dynasty ruling the whole of the Chinese world.

The triumph in 221 B.C.E. stemmed from long internal evolution in Ch'in territory of new political forms, which were now extended over the whole country. This is considered the last "revolution" in Chinese political history until the early twentieth century. It replaced feudal decentralization with a new imperial state wherein all areas were ruled directly from the capital. Feudal lords were replaced by bureaucrats —dependent servants of the central ruler—who carried out his orders and collected taxes. To signify this departure from past practice, the Ch'in ruler called himself Emperor (*Huang-ti*) instead of King (*Wang*), the title that had been used by Chou rulers and usurped by various feudal strongmen during the centuries of conflict.

The final ingredient in the political theory of legitimate rule was added when the Ch'in dynasty fell in 206 B.C.E. in a peasant rebellion. Former emperors, kings, and feudal lords had all stemmed from old aristocratic families and had partially based their claims to power on their descent from ancient noble lineages. The peasant leader of the rebellion in 206 B.C.E. could make no such claim. Although religious myths were fabricated to explain his conception, religious sanction for a change of ruling house had to be reinterpreted. Thereafter, it was argued that a new line of emperors achieved political power, not by crass military might or because of aristocratic lineage, but by Heaven's Mandate rewarding ethical superiority. Divine support was demonstrated by the people's acceptance of the victorious regime.

A glance at the chronological chart will indicate that central rule was frequently interrupted, particularly during the Periods of Disunity when short-lived dynasties controlled only parts of China. The chart, however, does not show all of the periods of division. For example, after 1127 the Sung dynasty actually controlled only the southern portion of the country, while various foreign rulers controlled all or portions of north China. The ideal of unified control never died out, however. For two thousand years the desirable norm remained a unified country under the direct authority of an emperor. Any deviation, it was hoped, would prove short-lived.

The flexibility of the Heaven's Mandate theory permitted even non-Chinese to rule. The Mongols in the thirteenth and fourteenth centuries ruled China as Chinese emperors, but the best example of foreign rule was the Ch'ing or Manchu dynasty (1644–1911), the last in the long series of dynasties. The Manchus were a non-Chinese tribal people in the area later called Manchuria, just outside the political boundaries of the reigning Ming dynasty (1368–1644). Early in the seventeenth century, an enterprising Manchu chieftain called Nurhachi began to unify the dispersed tribal clans that made up the Manchu people. He did this, in part, by deliberately importing Chinese political institutions, practices, and laws. Chinese officials, fleeing from political persecution in China, found employment as advisers in the new Manchu court. When the tottering Ming dynasty fell in a peasant rebellion in 1643, the Manchu armies moved into north China on the invitation of a Chinese general who preferred foreign rulers to the rebel mob in the capital city of Peking. After suppressing the uprising, the Manchus set themselves up as rulers. They claimed political legitimacy under the traditional Mandate theory which, despite the Chinese sense of cultural superiority, made no racial distinctions and required only that a dynasty maintain the values of Chinese culture. Although careful to preserve privileged status for their own small numbers, the Manchus ruled China in the traditional Chinese manner.

Political Practice

Central to the entire governmental structure was the "Son of Heaven," as the emperor was frequently called. Theoretically, all policy decisions had to come directly from him. The great imperial seal or the emperor's personal handwriting on a document were the sole symbols of authority, and there was no provision or room for division of powers. He was the lone executive, sole legislator, and supreme judge. He was also expected to possess both the wisdom to decide the nation's religious and philosophical beliefs and the aesthetic ability to set high standards in art, literature, music, and other areas of culture. Obviously, the demands of the office required a level of talent and dedication that few of its occupants could come close to meeting.

A bureaucracy carried out the actual administration of the emperor's authority. From its beginnings even before Ch'in-Han times, the bureaucratic arm of government gradually grew in size, complexity, and importance. While the militant Ch'in emperor had used army commanders as bureaucrats, succeeding Han emperors started the recruitment of non-aristocrats. Picked for their education, talent, and loyalty to the emperor, these non-aristocratic bureaucrats could be depended upon to check the ambitions of other bureaucrats chosen from imperial relatives, generals, or powerful members of the aristocracy.

Recruitment according to education and talent rather than privilege and birth was a potentially revolutionary idea, one which took centuries to mature. Begun in the Han period, it was taken up by later rulers who developed, after the seventh century, an elaborate civil-service examination system. The idea of choosing government officials by an impartial testing of abilities may not seem revolutionary today. Within its own time period, however, the Chinese examination system was unique. It ultimately became the inspiration for our own civil-service examinations. Never completely devoid of corruption, the Chinese examination system nevertheless did provide government with the majority, and certainly with the most distinguished, of its administrators during the last thousand years of the imperial system.

Under the examination system of the Ming and Ch'ing dynasties, three levels of formal examinations took place, each with a separate degree granted to successful candidates. Candidates were initially screened at the county level to qualify for formal written competitions, held two out of every three years at the local prefectural capital.

Success at this level brought recognition to a candidate as one of the educated élite, or *literati* class, entitled to certain privileges such as exemption from labour taxes. Most important, however, possession of this lower-level degree was required for social acceptance as a bona fide member of the "gentry"; landownership, wealth, and family lineage were not sufficient unless in each generation a family member succeeded in the examinations. To retain this lower-degree status, the candidate had either to submit to periodic re-examination or pass on to the next level, the triennial examinations at each provincial capital. Thousands participated in these elaborate testing sessions, yet usually less than one per cent were successful. Provincial success made one eligible to compete in the final stage, the triennial metropolitan examinations held at the national capital. The successful candidates at this final testing represented the country's highest academic achievers and formed the pool of bureaucrats for official posting within the government. At all levels, quotas were used to achieve some rough geo-

Examination System
(simplified for Ch'ing period, 1644–1911)

Administrative Level	Path of Successful Candidates	Degree Sought
Imperial Palace		(final ranking of *chin-shih* and appointment to bureaucratic posts)
Metropolitan Capital (Peking)		*chin-shih* ("presented scholar")
Province (*sheng*) 18 in number		*chü-jen* ("recommended man")
Prefecture (*fu*) c. 180 in number		*hsiu-ts'ai* ("flowering talent")
County (*hsien*) c. 1300 in number		(screening of candidates by local educational authorities)

graphic representation from each area. Official degrees were sometimes granted without examination to sons of eminent officials, and some lower-level degrees were also available by purchase. These permitted the holder to gain the social recognition of gentry status, although neither political office nor the clearly higher prestige of the scholar's examination success were available to purchasers of degrees.

In the seventeenth century a European visitor to China, Matteo Ricci, described the provincial-level examinations in the following manner:

> There is an immense palace built especially for this examination in every metropolitan city, closed in by a great wall. In it there are a number of suites, secluded from all distraction, which are assigned to the examiners. . . . In the center of this palace there are more than four thousand small cells, just large enough to contain a small table and a seat for one person. The cells are so constructed that the occupant cannot converse with the one in the next compartment, or even see him. . . . During that particular time, both night and day, a guard of magistrates and of military sentinels is in continual circulation to prevent all contact by word or by writing between those who are engaged in the palace and those outside.
>
> The same three days are set aside for this examination throughout the kingdom, namely—the ninth, the twelfth, and fifteenth of the eighth moon. Those taking part in the examinations are permitted to write from dawn to sunset, behind locked doors, and they are served with light meals, prepared the day before at public expense. When the candidate bachelors are admitted to the palace, they are carefully searched to see that they have no book or written matter in their possession. Entering the examination, they are allowed to have several brushes for writing, the writer's palette, and also ink and paper. Their clothes and even the brushes and palettes are carefully examined lest they should contain anything deceitful, and if fraud of any kind is discovered they are not only excluded from the examination but are severely punished as well.
>
> . . .
>
> . . . Each one must also recopy his [examination] manuscript into a copybook prepared for that purpose and at the end of the dissertation, in addition to his own name, he signs the names of his parents, grandparents, and his great-grandparents. Then the book is so sealed that it can be opened only by the Deputies. Each one does this with as many copybooks as he may have used, and he presents them personally to the Deputy. These books are again recopied by the librarians or by amanuenses appointed for

that purpose. To prevent any partiality, the books are marked with a particular character in red, before they are presented to the examiners, and the autographs are omitted. These manuscripts, without autographs, are the ones that are submitted to the examiners for rating. The autographed copies are numbered to correspond with the markings on the manuscript presented. This method is followed to prevent recognition of the manuscripts and to conceal the author's identity and his handwriting in the formation of the script characters.[5]

The content of the examinations tested one's memory of certain Confucian classics, standard histories, and a limited scope of allied literary texts. Inflexible as to what was considered acceptable style and handwriting, and intolerant of anything but orthodox doctrines, the examinations still meant that the civil service was staffed by scholars, men who had the mental stamina to endure long years of training in classical studies of philosophy, history, and literature.

The bureaucratic structure spread downward from its apex, the omnipotent emperor. At the capital, advisory bodies assisted him in making policy decisions. These were in turn administered by the bureaucracy, which had three main divisions. One group of bureaus and ministries oversaw various aspects of civil administration, and a similar, though smaller, group of offices oversaw military affairs. Both civil and military streams had separate examination systems for potential recruits. These two bureaucracies were supplemented by a third, a unique institution called the censorate. It was responsible for detecting and reporting any malpractice or corruption within the other two branches. In keeping with this ominous responsibility, censors were usually drawn from among the most highly principled and worthy bureaucrats in the other two branches. The triad of civil, military, and censorial bureaucracies at the capital was duplicated within each provincial administration, and all came together only at the top, within the person of the emperor himself.

The civil branch was by far the largest of the three. Early in the evolution of the system, military commanders, particularly in peripheral posts on China's frontiers, often operated independently of central government control, sometimes endangering the throne itself. The founder of the Sung dynasty (960–1279) was himself raised to the throne as leader of a successful army revolt, but he determined to curb the military's threat to civil power. Although faced with threatened invasions from superior non-Chinese forces along the northern frontiers, he instituted changes which thereafter placed the Chinese military under the authority of the civil bureaucracy. While military leaders were certainly prominent in later imperial history, total civil dominance over military power became an ideal of the traditional Chinese system. This also had important social consequences as careers in the military became much less prestigious than certain civilian pursuits.

We must not lose perspective of China's sheer size in relation to all this elaborate structure. Beyond the sustenance of the imperial family and the government, the political structure was concerned mainly with the securing of peace and stability. Internal and external security, the collection of taxes, and the building and maintenance of public works for irrigation and flood control comprised the bulk of administrative activity. Even in these functions, the official government's role was largely supervisory. The lowest official government representative was the magistrate of a *hsien*, or county; he was the one man responsible for all the affairs of as many as half a million people. Administrative details at the local level were handled primarily by the non-bureaucratic local gentry. Educated in the same conservative principles as the officials, the neighbourhood gentry directed local affairs, settled most local disputes, organized local public-works projects, and acted as a buffer between the magistrate and the peasant population. Compared to our modern governments, this traditional bureaucratic system was limited in function and in size. In the nineteenth century, its 28 000 officials handled all formal government matters for a population of about 300 million people.

Analysis

1. The system of government instituted and developed by the emperors was admirably effective because it was compatible with existing social and economic conditions. Discuss the validity of this statement.

2. At what stage or stages in a country's development is a centralized autocratic government desirable? At what stage or stages is a liberal democratic regime desirable? Defend your answers with specific examples.

Suggested Readings

C. O. Hucker, *The Traditional Chinese State in Ming Times (1368–1644)* (Tucson: University of Arizona Press, 1961).
   An excellent, detailed short summary of institutions and practices of the late imperial structure.

E. A. Kracke, Jr., "The Chinese and the Art of Government," in R. Dawson, ed., *The Legacy of China* (London and New York: Oxford University Press, 1964), 309–39.
   A stimulating short essay on the key institutional practices of traditional Chinese government.

J. M. Menzel, ed., *The Chinese Civil Service: Career Open to Talent?* (Boston: Heath, 1963).
   A good selection of various readings around the question of the examination system's effects on Chinese social mobility, with a good bibliography for further readings.

F. Michael, "State and Society in 19th Century China," in A. Feuerwerker, ed., *Modern China* (Englewood Cliffs, N.J.: Prentice-Hall, 1964), 57–69.
   A good general analysis of the interaction between political and social structure of late imperial China.

CHAPTER 4
The Intellectual Framework of Traditional China

Ideas and traditions passed on from generation to generation represent an essential part of any culture. Variations in religious beliefs, philosophical ideals, and social and economic values may separate the élite and the commoners in a particular society. But certain of these beliefs, ideals, and values are likely to be shared by all members of a culture, and it is these elements held in common that distinguish members of one culture from another. To understand China's history, an examination of the major features of its traditional patterns of thought is essential.

A word of caution is immediately required. Throughout their long history, the Chinese characteristically preferred to avoid making sharp distinctions between systems of thought. For example, no clear line was drawn between religious and secular philosophy; all bodies of ideas were simply labelled "teachings." Both individually and collectively, the Chinese did demonstrate preferences for some "isms" over others, but in so doing they tended to blend rather freely the features of various teachings. Thus, when we discuss separately the various "isms," we should remember that the Chinese looked at these more as interrelated aspects of a single body of ideas than as distinct philosophies from which a single choice must be made. A simple example: a single Chinese funeral ceremony could involve both Taoist and Buddhist priests, and it was with surprise that the Chinese received the early western Christian missionaries' refusal to be included as a third element within the religious practices surrounding the burial of a beloved member of the family.

To further illustrate this blending tendency and to introduce the terms required for discussing traditional Chinese philosophies, we might try to imagine a typical Chinese scholar-official of late imperial times. Such an individual could be described in the following manner (an elaboration of the italicized terms will come in the pages below). Educated in *Confucian* classics, he served in an imperial bureaucracy under an emperor-centred system developed through the theory of *Legalism*. When seeking temporary relief from official duties, and later, when as a retired gentleman he was freed of responsibility, he took a *Taoist* attitude toward life. Finally, concerned with the question of life-after-death, this same gentleman incorporated strands of *Buddhism* into his thought.

Of course, such a pattern was not typical of all periods of Chinese history, or of all members of the scholar-official class at any one time. However, countless examples through the ages suggest that this bringing together of different philosophic and religious beliefs was a basic characteristic of the psychology of traditional China.

Much of our discussion revolves around ideas originating in the late Chou period (from the eighth to the third century B.C.E.), an era of political and social unrest accompanying the decay of the feudal structure. Major economic changes were taking place. Large-scale irrigation projects, the development of fertilizers, and the introduction of the iron-tipped plough allowed increased yields, and therefore greater population concentrations. In the absence of a strong central government, ambitious feudal aristocrats sought to harness the new wealth and to increase their own power. At the same time, the nature of warfare changed: large armies of peasant foot-soldiers replaced smaller forces of chariot-borne aristocrats. Warfare also became less of a "polite" occupation. Conflict now was not over questions of honour or the glory of one's noble clan, but over the acquisition of territory and the control of people. In this turbulent age were laid the foundations of later Chinese thought.

In response to the problems of the age, great numbers of thinkers sought both individual and collective solutions. Many wandered from feudal court to feudal court in search of intellectual exchange and stimulation, as well as sponsors to implement their schemes. Confucianism, Taoism, and Legalism, the major schools of later Chinese philosophy, emerged from the Hundred Schools of Thought, a term used loosely to cover the many contending philosophies of this period. Most of these schools of thought were forgotten, although many of their ideas were absorbed into the three surviving systems. The only major addition of later times was Buddhism, a religious philosophy of great influence, which first flourished in the chaotic times following the fall of the Han dynasty in the early third century C.E. Later centuries were by no means lacking in intellectual excitement, but the chief categories of philosophical and religious debate within China were set in these early years.

Legalism

Of all the Hundred Schools of Thought, Legalism is perhaps the least attractive to modern minds and therefore the least known of Chinese traditional philosophies. Indeed, it also proved unattractive to later Chinese writers. Its contribution to the imperial system, however, was equally as great as that of its two main rivals, Taoism and Confucianism, and traces of its influence can be found right down to modern times.

Legalism was a political philosophy. Its answer to the upheavals of late Chou times was a totalitarian state. Legalist philosophers maintained that peace and security could come only by universal application of a perfected set of laws. Once such law codes existed, they would be made universal, without privilege or exemption for any individual or group. The swiftness of justice and the certainty of harsh punishments for offenders would frighten all people into submission and obedience, resulting in a peaceful and orderly society. This could happen only under a single political ruler with absolute authority. Military discipline was to be the model for social order, just as military power was the proposed weapon to forge this new state. The Legalists (whom some writers have preferred to label Realists) looked upon all talk of higher principles as a sign of weakness or stupidity. Only power —unified, centralized, and total—really counted. All people, as well as ideas, were judged in terms of what they contributed to the strengthening of state control.

These ideas became the official philosophy of the state of Ch'in. While still only one of several contending feudal kingdoms during the late Chou period, Ch'in organized just such a society. In contrast with other parts of the country, Ch'in constructed a social system in which military prowess, rather than wealth or noble birth, brought social prestige. Ch'in's military organization embraced the entire population; women and old men formed a defensive force for the home area while the regular armies were elsewhere in search of new conquests. Economic resources were totally mobilized in the service of the ruler rather than for individual benefit. The resultant accumulation of power enabled Ch'in to survive in the harsh interstate warfare of the fourth and third centuries B.C.E., eventually to conquer all its rivals, and to emerge as the single ruler of all China.

Ch'in's universal rule lasted less than two decades, but the ambitious programs launched by Legalist advisers to the emperor during those few years left a legacy that remained long after rebellions ended the dynasty in 206 B.C.E. These advisers believed that absolute unity was required for perpetuating the new political regime. This led to the establishment of a unified writing style for Chinese characters, the building of a system of roads and other communications networks radiating out from the capital at Hsien-yang, and the standardizing of weights, measures, and currency. These policies were forcibly implemented under the emperor's absolute authority.

Two specific examples illustrate the ruthlessness and authoritarianism of Legalist philosophy. The vibrant exchange of ideas by wandering philosophers during late Chou times was, in the eyes of the Legalists, a potential source of danger to the new system. They believed that if all China was to remain one state, one school of thought must prevail. Li Ssu (d. 208 B.C.E.), chief spokesman for the

Legalist advisers, put the case before the Ch'in emperor in this way:

> Therefore I, your minister, propose that all histories, except the official history of the Ch'in state, should be burned. . . . Those who dare to criticize the present regime by invoking the ancient writings should be likewise put to death, together with all members of their families. Government officials who know that violations have occurred but choose not to prosecute would be regarded as having committed the same crime as that committed by the offenders. If books are not burned thirty days after the order has been issued, the offenders should have their faces branded and should be exiled to the northern frontier to build the Great Wall.[6]

In 213 B.C.E. this policy was carried out. State officials collected and destroyed whatever books they found in private hands, except those pertaining to agriculture or the history of the Ch'in state.

The Great Wall of China, stretching more than 1 600 kilometres across north China, was another symbol of Ch'in autocracy and drive for unity. A grand scheme, undertaken to link together the previously separate and incomplete fortifications of several feudal states, the sheer size of the undertaking demonstrated the power of the new imperial state. The Wall physically separated the nomadic cultures of the northern tribal peoples from the intensive agricultural settlements of the Chinese. It protected the latter against raiding parties and also locked the Chinese peasant into the new state structure. The Wall is sometimes called "the longest cemetery in the world," in recognition of the thousands of labourers who died in its construction. These casualties included many intellectuals, condemned to construction gangs for expressing criticisms of the Ch'in order.

The life of the Ch'in autocracy was brief. A loose alliance of displaced aristocratic remnants, disgruntled scholars, and repressed peasantry united against it in several simultaneous rebellions. After the overthrow, the Chinese intellectual class recovered rapidly from the attempt to reduce all "isms" to a single pattern of thought. Legalism, as a distinct intellectual school, disappeared in the popular revulsion against Ch'in repression, and the writings of other schools of thought were restored, either from hidden copies of books or from the

Great Public Works of Traditional China

The Great Wall, extending across north China from the Pacific to the far northwest, initially completed by the Ch'in dynasty (upper); the Grand Canal, connecting the Yangtze basin with north China, initially completed by the Sui dynasty (lower).

memories of living scholars. However, the Burning of the Books and the Great Wall remained etched in the memories of later Chinese intellectuals. They never forgot the political and intellectual consequences of Legalist totalitarian ideology.

Legalism's effects continued, however, despite its disappearance as a co-ordinated school of thought. The Chinese Empire, a united China ruled directly from a single locale of power, and the emperor, the unchallenged centre of political authority, were its creations, and both lasted until the twentieth century. After the Ch'in period, the capital city was the nation's centre and the emperor was the unchallengeable source of decision.

In another sense as well, Legalism's influence coloured later centuries, for Chinese society retained an almost universal distaste for the concept of living by the strict letter of a single written code of law. Laws did exist, collected in elaborate codes and commentaries, but these related primarily to criminal and administrative matters. No body of civil or commercial law was drawn up. An extremely practical people, the Chinese believed that laws and punishments were necessary to guarantee order in society, but they always viewed these as unfortunate necessities. Any reliance on legal arguments, by either officials or private subjects, was an admission of failure—failure to govern by persuasive moral example rather than force, or failure on the part of an individual to live by the ideal of social harmony rather than individual self-interest. "Legalist" became a derogatory, even insulting term, hurled at one's political opponents much in the manner that "fascist" appears in heated political debates in our own time.

Taoism or The School of the Way

The Tao [Way] that can be told of
  Is not the eternal Tao;
The name that can be named
  Is not the eternal name.
Nameless, it is the origin of Heaven and earth;
Namable, it is the mother of all things.

Always nonexistent,
  That we may apprehend its inner secret;

Always existent,
That we may discern its outer manifestations.
These two are the same;
Only as they manifest themselves they receive different names.[7]

Taoism, as a school of ideas, took shape in the same late Chou period. The great names associated with Taoism are Lao-tzu ("Old Master"), who is supposed to have lived in the sixth century B.C.E. but probably is a mythical figure, and Chuang-tzu ("Master Chuang") whose traditional dates are 369–268 B.C.E.

Taoist writers counselled philosophical detachment rather than activist participation in the turbulent political world of their time:

To seek learning one gains day by day;
To seek the Tao one loses day by day.
    Losing and yet losing some more,
    Till one has reached doing nothing [*wu-wei*].
Do nothing and yet there is nothing that is not done.
To win the world one must attend to nothing.
When one attends to this and that,
    He will not win the world.[8]

Taoists ridiculed any conscious effort, collectively, or individually, to create and maintain prestige, wealth, power, or, in effect, any material goal.

Once Chuang Tzu was fishing in the P'u River when the King of Ch'u sent two of his ministers to announce that he wished to entrust to Chuang Tzu the care of his entire domain.

Chuang Tzu held his fishing pole and, without turning his head, said: "I have heard that Ch'u possesses a sacred tortoise which has been dead for three thousand years and which the king keeps wrapped up in a box and stored in his ancestral temple. Is this tortoise better off dead and with its bones venerated, or would it be better off alive with its tail dragging in the mud?"

"It would be better off alive and dragging its tail in the mud," the two ministers replied.

"Then go away!" said Chuang Tzu, "and I will drag my tail in the mud!"[9]

Rejecting social prestige and political or military power as worthy human aspirations, Taoists praised the effortless life and proclaimed the joys of total harmony with one's fellows. Unconcerned with questions of human fortune or of an organized society, they sought personal detachment from the struggles of social existence, and some even preached total withdrawal from society.

Against seeking material gain, they upheld the simple pleasures of appreciating and identifying with the harmony of nature. From the natural world came many of their most striking analogies—the twisted, knotty old tree on a wind-swept mountain peak, whose very uselessness to humanity enabled it to survive, or still water, whose tranquillity hid its capacity to eventually wear down all solid matter. In a perfectly balanced nature, Taoists saw their ideal—the Tao, or Way. Individuals should try to follow the Way as manifested in the awe-inspiring regularity of nature's processes, seen as a constant pattern of effortless creation and unemotional dying, all in perfect harmony.

These ideas had considerable impact on both the political and cultural traditions of China. In contrast to Legalism, Taoism's political message was *laissez-faire* government—the less done the better—and this often led its proponents close to outright anarchism. In contrast to the rigid moral preachings of the Confucians, Taoism advocated pure, often totally uninhibited, personal indulgence in the "natural" pleasures of life, free of any socially or politically imposed standards. These views were particularly favoured by those who were already inclined to rebel against established social norms, and even in the sober prose of official histories (written primarily by Confucians), sufficient notice is made of such "eccentrics" to indicate their colour and liveliness. Taoism's greatest influence was on Chinese literary and artistic tradition. Chinese art and poetry reflect especially Taoism's stress on humanity's oneness with nature.

Taoism also muted the effects of fatalism which, in early China, as in other agricultural cultures, had grown from the harsh realities of a life dependent on the unpredictable course of nature. Taoists cherished life and looked upon periodic setbacks of existence as inevitable. Life, and eventually death itself, were part of the benevolent cosmos of nature. By making even human failure part of the natural order,

Lao-Tzu, "Old Master" of Taoism, riding into wilderness on water-buffalo; bronze statue, uncertain date.

Taoism softened its emotional impact—one failed, not necessarily because of one's shortcomings, but because failure was natural when one strove to succeed. True wisdom, or "enlightenment," lay not in trying to better one's position by either book learning or competition with others, but in acquiring the psychological ability to accept either success or failure with calm.

These philosophical and aesthetic perspectives particularly affected the educated Chinese élite, but Taoism also had a religious side which was more evident on the popular level. The label "religious Taoism" came to include many diverse ideas which, even at a superficial glance, had little to do with the original Taoist outlook on life. Religious Taoism's central focus was the search for longevity and immortality. Some practitioners set out, through alchemy, to discover an elixir for long life. The results were not insignificant for science; although emperors and empresses sometimes died from imbibing one of the many potions for immortality, such experiments were also responsible for some early Chinese discoveries in medicine and in other scientific fields. Various schools of religious Taoists fostered the notion of inner hygiene in the search for longevity, through health practices ranging from simple diets to yoga-type discipline, meditative contemplation, or the sequence of exercises we call Chinese shadow-boxing. Belief in the supernatural permeated the various schools of religious Taoism. This included trust in the magical powers of true believers, and a belief in the Immortals (former followers of the Way who had found the secret of immortality and lived forever on some far-off island in the Pacific Ocean).

Religious Taoist sects attracted many adherents, particularly among the peasantry. Popular novels and folk tales clearly reflect Taoist influences. The strength of Taoism among the people is suggested by the evidence of frequent official concern, the government tending to look upon any unofficial public grouping, and particularly a religious one, as potentially dangerous. Nor was such a fear unfounded, as many a peasant rebellion was encouraged by Taoist assurance of supernatural protection for its forces.

Confucianism

Confucianism was the most famous of the three great philosophies stemming from the late Chou period. Among the great thinkers who, through the centuries, contributed to its development, the three most honoured were Confucius (550–479 B.C.E.), Mencius (372–289 B.C.E.), and Chu Hsi (1130–1200 C.E.). The philosophy that is associated with their names became synonymous with traditional Chinese society and culture. In political history, we speak of the "Confucian monarchy" and the "Confucian examination system." Both private and public morality were based on the Confucian family and on Confucian values. Confucianism is both credited with the strengths of traditional Chinese society and blamed for its supposed static quality.

Confucius lived during the chaotic period of the late Chou. Born in the feudal state of Lu (in modern Shantung province), he was well educated as a youth, suggesting that he came from a minor aristocratic background rather than the more humble origins he claimed. He apparently held relatively unimportant political offices in the Lu bureaucracy before he became, at the age of sixty, the typical wandering philosopher-scholar in search of a feudal court that would employ his talents. Ten years later he returned to Lu, without having found his ideal prince; nor had he received any offers of a post in which he might put his political ideas into practice. It should be noted that this man who became the patron saint of Chinese bureaucracy did not himself have a brilliant administrative career. Most of his life was spent in study and teaching. He is remembered above all as the first professional teacher, and one who, in an aristocratic age, opened his classroom to anyone of talent, whatever his social background.

Elaborated upon over the centuries by scholars, the core of Confucianism rested on certain premises established by its founder. Foremost was his insistence on the inseparability of morality and politics. Confucius also taught a profound respect for recorded history as the repository of human values. It was from history that a ruler could deduce the necessary doctrines to assure proper, peaceful rule, and these doctrines were moral lessons rather than political techniques or military strategies. Confucius laid great stress on the value of collective existence and the search for harmonious social and political frameworks within which ethical behaviour, rather than naked force or personal profit, would prevail. He stressed the basic importance of the family and proclaimed the necessity of moral behaviour in the political and social spheres. Society, in his eyes, was merely an oversized family. In both family and society, one ought to follow a highly regulated pattern of behaviour, according to one's assigned social role. Confucius believed that if everyone followed these defined codes of conduct, both family and society would be harmonious.

He looked back to a Golden Age—the Sage-King era, a period in ancient history well before the Shang dynasty—when sages, or rulers of outstanding virtue, had supposedly reigned without harsh laws, elaborate military establishments, or heavy taxes. The lessons of that period were clear: in the ideal society, the sovereign was benevolent, the subject obedient; the father was paternalistic, the son energetic in the practice of filial devotion to the wishes and welfare of his parents; the husband was kind, the wife chaste and obedient; the elder brother

Confucius; stone engraving, Ch'ing period.

was a guide, the younger brother a pupil; and friends were mutually respectful. If the élite of society adopted these virtues, Confucius believed, the lower levels would respond to their good example and the happiness of that ancient period of perfection would be recaptured. Finally, Confucius reinforced the basic conservatism of his thinking by claiming to be only a transmitter of this ancient legacy, rather than a creator of new philosophical principles.

Mencius, the "Second Sage" of Confucianism, looked upon his own contributions as elaborations of Confucius' interpretations of the sage-kings' wisdom. Mencius particularly stressed that government existed for the people's welfare:

> Here is the way to win the empire: win the people and you win the empire.
> Here is the way to win the people: win their hearts and you win the people.
> Here is the way to win their hearts: give them and share with them what

they like, and do not do to them what they do not like. The people turn to a humane ruler as water flows downward or beasts take to wilderness.[10]

Government was thus judged by its humaneness rather than by its wealth, courtly elegance, or military exploits. Mencius insisted that all people were born innately good, turning to evil only when society failed to encourage goodness. An ethical ruler, governing by moral example, would influence the masses and enable them to follow their natural instincts for goodness.

In a passage of his writings often regarded by later Chinese emperors as bordering on subversion, Mencius continued this line of thought, giving to Confucianism a particular twist of the old concept of Heaven's Mandate to rule. In speaking of the right of one of the ancient sage-kings to the throne, he noted:

> He was appointed to preside over the sacrifices, and all the spirits were pleased with them: that indicated his acceptance by Heaven. He was placed in charge of public affairs, and they were well administered and the people were at peace: that indicated his acceptance by the people. Heaven thus gave him the empire; the people thus gave him the empire.[11]

In this championing of the common people, Mencius seemed to advocate their inherent right of rebellion against tyrannical rulers. He was no democrat or revolutionary in the modern sense, but he did infuse into Confucianism a strong sense of identification with popular welfare. At least amongst the highly principled members of the later scholar-official class, this often meant confrontation with the Legalist-minded emperors they served.

Confucianism did not become a dominant school of thought during Confucius' or even Mencius' time, or for some time afterwards. In the chaotic military politics of the late Chou period, its practitioners earned the title of *Ju*, or weaklings, perhaps indicating how contemporaries viewed their call for a virtuous rather than a powerful ruler and state. However, basic Confucian ideas struck responsive chords in Chinese society. Beginning in the Han period, commoners were recruited for the imperial bureaucracy on the basis of literary and ethical qualities. Personal integrity, and the dedication to government service with which students of Confucianism were imbued, proved attractive to emperors. The Confucian insistence on the unity of intellectual, moral, and political life gradually came to fruition with the perfection of the examination system a thousand years after the fall of the Han. In the last centuries of imperial times, to be educated meant being trained almost exclusively in the Confucian classics; to be a government official one had to pass the rigorous exams that tested one's grasp of Confucian principles.

Over the centuries Confucianism did change. Confucius looked at the world from the perspective of one who lived in an aristocratic society, and even Mencius' perceptions were limited by the decentralized feudalism of his age. For example, on the question of man's relationship to the spirit world or the origins of the universe, a few comments made by Confucius himself typify the original Confucian attitude:

> Tzu Lu asked about the worship of ghosts and spirits. Confucius said: "We don't know yet how to serve men, how can we know about serving the spirits?" "What about death," was the next question. Confucius said: "We don't know yet about life, how can we know about death?"
>
> Fan Ch'ih asked about wisdom. Confucius said: "Devote yourself to the proper demands of the people, respect the ghosts and spirits but keep them at a distance—this may be called wisdom."
>
> The Master did not talk about weird things, physical exploits, disorders, and spirits.[12]

In the early Han period, Confucians had to adjust their ideas to the realities of a new imperial state, a new form of society, and new intellectual interests.

In the process, they adopted certain cosmological ideas belonging to other, non-Confucian modes of thought. Han Confucianism, for example, absorbed and developed the idea of *yin* (coldness, weakness, moon, femaleness) and *yang* (heat, strength, sun, maleness) as two original forces, or principles, of creation. All natural phenomena sprang from and changed according to the continuous interaction of the two cosmic principles of *yin* and *yang*. Far removed from the original ideas of Confucius, such later notions did not alter the major thrust of Confucianism, which remained consistent with its founder's prime concerns: how to achieve social and political stability through moral and educational rather than legalistic or military means.

Buddhism and Later Chinese Thought

Buddhism provides the only pre-modern example of extensive foreign influence on Chinese thought and thereby allows us to study how the Chinese adapted and absorbed an intellectual invader into their strong native tradition. This Indian religion stems from the life and thoughts of Gautama Buddha, the "historic Buddha," who lived in the sixth century B.C.E., or roughly at the same time as Confucius. Though many Buddhist sects developed, all believed that life was suffering, that suffering was caused by natural desires, and that the end of suffering came only with the final extinction of desires. Most Buddhist sects also preached the doctrine of continual reincarnation. The form of rebirth (male or female, human or animal) and the state into which one was reborn (lord or peasant, strong or weak) was determined by one's accumulations of merit or demerit in previous existences. Whatever the form or state, all life continued to be suffering until one was able to eliminate desires.

Buddhism held out the promise of ultimate personal salvation through escape from this endless cycle of pain. Escape was the achievement of Buddhahood—a state of perfected enlightenment, latent within oneself. Various sects differed in their proposed paths to salvation. These included monastic celibacy, demonstrations of piety and acts of public charity, belief in benevolent intervention by former "saints" called bodhisattvas, and rigorous programs of meditation to eliminate the causes of pain by overcoming one's mental barriers to enlightenment. Warm and compassionate in its religious idealism, and rich in literary and artistic forms, Buddhism's strong spiritual qualities posed a major challenge to the main thrust of Confucian and Taoist thought.

Buddhism initially flourished in China during and immediately following the decline of the Han dynasty (206 B.C.E.–220 C.E.). In this period, the classical empire created by the Ch'in unification and Han consolidation gave way to centuries of disunity, invasion by outsiders in the north, and constant internal struggles between domestic contenders for political power in the south. After the glories of the Han empire, the chaos that followed discredited traditional beliefs and made the new ideas of Buddhism attractive to both the élite and the commoners. When the empire was again unified under the Sui (589 – 618) and T'ang (618 – 906) dynasties, Buddhism had become the major religious force within Chinese society. Its temples and pagodas dotted the landscape, its monastic orders wielded considerable political and social influence, and its financial power, in the form of accumulated wealth and land, rivalled even the imperial treasury.

The wealth and influence of Buddhism evoked envy in official circles, while its dominance over intellectual activity aroused the opposition of both Taoists and Confucians. The result was a reaction against Buddhism by the traditional forces in society, now rejuvenated by the reunification of the empire. In 845, the emperor issued an edict

Buddhist pagoda in Soochow, originally built in twelfth century and rebuilt late in sixteenth century.

suppressing the independent power of Buddhist institutions:

> I have heard that there was no Buddhism before the Three Dynasties [i.e., pre-772 B.C.E.] and that it began to spread only after the Han and Wei [220–280 C.E.] dynasties. Slowly and gradually it spread; its adherents multiplied with the passage of time. . . . Manpower was wasted in temple building, and gold and other valuables which should have been people's private wealth were taken away to decorate Buddhist temples. Disregarding their duty towards their king and their parents, the monks and nuns pledged loyalty and obedience only to their Buddhist superiors. They violated the vow of matrimony by deserting their spouses so that they could abide by the so-called rules of [monastic] discipline. Nothing in the world was so harmful to man and his good customs as this alien belief called Buddhism.
>
> . . .
>
> When this measure takes effect, more than 4,600 temples will be demolished, and more than 260,500 monks and nuns will be returned to civilian life and registered as taxpayers. No less than 40,000 monasteries are also scheduled to be demolished. Moreover, good land amounting to hundreds and thousands of *ching* [1 *ching* is approx. 6 hectares] will be appropriated by the government, together with 150,000 male and female slaves, all of whom will be reclassified as taxpaying citizens.[13]

Thereafter, the government controlled the size of Buddhism's formal structure and prevented it from ever becoming anything like a national church system.

Simultaneously, Confucianism took strength from the reunified imperial culture and challenged Buddhism's hold on the intellectual class. This variation of classical Confucianism is known in the West as Neo-Confucianism (or, in Chinese, as the School of Reason). Finally formulated by Chu Hsi in the late twelfth century, it borrowed from both Taoism and Buddhism in tying human ethics and human concerns to the natural order of the universe. At the same time, its purpose was to reassert the reality and importance of living within society, as opposed to the Taoist rejection of human organizations and the Buddhist assertion of life's inevitable painfulness. During the last five hundred years of imperial China, to be educated meant to be schooled first in the Neo-Confucian secular concepts of how man should behave in a political and social framework.

Neither the civil authorities nor the Confucian thinkers sought to eradicate Buddhism once its institutions were weakened and its intellectual force blunted. The Buddhist faith continued as an individual belief, and remained the predominant religion of the masses. It retained its vitality for several centuries. On the scholastic level, the variety of Buddhism that sprang most obviously from its interaction with the native Chinese tradition appeared after the ninth-century persecutions. Known as the Meditative Sect, or Ch'an (and even better known as Zen, which is the Japanese pronunciation), it blended Buddhism with elements of Taoist thought in its philosophy of life. On the popular level of society, other Buddhist sects also engaged in free interaction and blending with religious Taoism, so that by late imperial times it was frequently impossible to distinguish which school of religious thought was the main inspiration for many local temples. Initially accepted to fill a spiritual vacuum in a period of social disruption, Buddhism survived by "nativization," becoming a part of the traditional Chinese culture. In so doing, it won a permanent place among Chinese philosophies.

Analysis

1. The author states that the Chinese "tended to blend rather freely the features of various teachings." What would be the advantages or disadvantages of merging various philosophies of life into one?

2. Supporters of Legalism have argued that a strong central government and very strict legal codes would bring about a harmonious society in which everyone would have a sense of place, security, purpose, and strength. Is this an ideal society? Why? Why not?

3. Was Legalism an early form of fascism? Would Legalism have been compatible with the ideology of Nazi Germany from 1933 to 1939?

4. Could Taoism provide a workable basis for a government? for a social organization?

5. Confucianism insisted on the "inseparability of morality and politics." Do you agree?

6. Mencius argued that government should be "judged by its humaneness." Do you agree?

7. How does one decide by what criteria to judge a government? Set up your own criteria for judging a government. Be prepared to defend each criterion.

8. Which of the philosophies of Legalism, Taoism, Buddhism, or Confucianism appeal to you? In what ways?

9. Could an individual be a Legalist, Taoist, Confucianist, and Buddhist at the same time?

10. Considering the basic philosophies common in China before the twentieth century, would Christian missionaries have had an easy time in converting the Chinese? Why? Why not?

Suggested Readings

H. G. Creel, *Chinese Thought from Confucius to Mao Tse-tung* (Chicago: University of Chicago Press, 1953).

    Authoritative, short general treatment of Chinese intellectual history.

A. Waley, ed., *Three Ways of Thought in Ancient China* (Garden City, N.Y.: Doubleday Anchor Books, 1956).

    Excellent introduction to Confucianism, Taoism, and "Realism" (i.e., Legalism) by means of extensive translations connected by informative commentary.

A. F. Wright, *Buddhism in Chinese History* (Stanford, Calif.: Stanford University Press, 1959).

    General history of Buddhism's effect on Chinese society and culture.

CHAPTER 5
Unity and Diversity in Traditional China

Before leaving traditional China to look at more modern times, one should recall its great achievement: the development and survival of a distinct and highly complex civilization. As we have briefly noted, through the centuries neighbouring groups (particularly nomadic tribal confederations on China's northern and northwestern borders) envied its riches. Despite constant raids and invasions, these outsiders never fundamentally altered the Chinese people's sense of their own unique culture and its continuity with their ancestors' past greatness. From other neighbouring cultures (particularly Korea, Japan, and North Vietnam), the Chinese civilization received the greatest compliment: imitation, or adoption of Chinese elements into their own societies at various times. Despite the diversity within China, despite the ebbing and flowing of its political fortunes, being "Chinese" provided a bond of common identity—with those living and with the past—which could overcome all challenges. Yet it is important to understand the variety of life and thought within this unity, and this chapter will briefly underline how internal diversities enriched Chinese civilization.

Food

The geographic variations and agricultural techniques discussed in earlier chapters demonstrate some of the basic diversities in both traditional and contemporary China. With so many regional crop differences and regional tastes, Chinese cuisine achieved a fascinating breadth. Fish and other marine life formed a specialty of the south, with very distinctive provincial and local variations in their preparation. Rice, a southern crop, was eaten throughout China, but its high cost in the northern provinces made it a common dish only in the diet of the rich. In north China, the cuisine centred on wheat-based foods, including noodles, which supposedly so impressed Marco Polo that he introduced pasta into the Italian diet. Some foodstuffs, such as sweet potatoes, peanuts, and soy-bean curd, were found in all areas, though prepared in different ways. In general, southern regions tended to favour sweeter foods, the northern regions preferred saltier tastes, while western provinces favoured hot, spicy specialties quite distinct from the milder dishes of the east. Food was eaten with chopsticks, which go far back in Chinese history.

Beverages were always served hot. The most common drink was water, and a cup of plain hot water may still today be offered to a foreign visitor in many peasant homes. Tea was used first as a medicine and then as a social beverage, and with its gradual spread came a wide range of types and blends for various tastes. Wine was most commonly made from rice and was also consumed hot. Several distinct varieties of liqueur-type beverages were developed, depending on the local base material. Beer is a modern import, and milk, as noted earlier, was widely used only by nomadic peoples in the far northwest. In short, while "Chinese" food has commonly-shared and unmistakably unique characteristics, it has within its scope a vast range of type, taste, and texture probably unmatched by any other national cuisine.

Language

Language provided another example of variations within a common Chinese culture. Some of the regional dialects differed only slightly in pronunciation and stress, somewhat similar to the differences between the accents in various parts of the English-speaking world. Others, however, represented linguistic differences as distinct as French, Spanish, and English. The only dialect spoken nation-wide was the "officials' speech" used by the educated élite. This had considerable political and social effects. A standard rule of Chinese bureaucratic posting was the so-called law of avoidance, which forbade the assignment of government officials to their home regions. This protection against favouritism often meant that officials had to serve in regions where the everyday speech was like a foreign language. For example, a northerner assigned to a southern province had to rely very heavily upon the local educated élite—the gentry of the region—who could speak both the local dialect and the "officials' speech."

While spoken language was strongly regional, the written language transcended such barriers to comprehension. Unity in the written language was possible because Chinese is written in characters—i.e., individual symbols representing a single idea or concept—rather than an alphabet that relies upon combinations of letters to construct various meanings. For example, Chinese compass directions are written as follows:

North 北 East 東 South 南 West 西 However one pronounces the character 北 , its meaning remains *north*. So long as both parties to a "conversation" can write, there was (and is) no need for them to struggle to catch every word of the other's unfamiliar dialect.

The written language also possessed other features that influenced the traditional culture. In sharp contrast to our own linguistic history, the separation of the written form from pronunciation meant that Chinese writing maintained a unique historical continuity, independent of changes in oral speech over the centuries. Put simply, in China (as in the West), the eighth-century oral language would be incomprehensible to an eighteenth-century individual. But while we sometimes have difficulty with Shakespeare (1564–1616) and need specialized training to read Chaucer (c. 1340–1400) in the original, eighth-century written Chinese was basically the same language as that in which an educated eighteenth-century Chinese wrote his civil-service examinations, composed poetry, and communicated with emperor or friend. With only minor difficulties, such a person could and did read the works of Confucius or Mencius. This strongly contrasts with an educated individual of the West who would have to learn an early form of his own language, plus Latin and Greek and possibly some languages of the ancient Near East, to study the origins of his civilization.

The social impact of such a linguistic history was significant, for it made education a monumental undertaking. To achieve basic literacy alone required the memorization of thousands of characters. Beyond this initial hurdle, it took further years of concentrated study to understand literary works reflecting centuries of sophisticated interpretations. Chinese intellectuals delighted in obscure literary allusions referring back to ancient texts, and with only a few characters they could suggest very complex ideas. This meant that to become a "literate" person (in the sense of being able to read and write at a level accepted as "intellectual"), it was necessary to spend long years becoming familiar with a vast body of literature. Traditional Chinese culture was highly literary. Profound respect for the written language was exemplified by a high regard for elegant calligraphy (the technique of drawing the characters), and this became an important art form. It has been suggested that in the late eighteenth century, more books existed in Chinese than in all other languages of the world combined. The difficulties in grasping this elaborate written language and literature made education a process reserved for only those with both perseverance and financial resources. The written language thus helped to separate society sharply into the educated élite and the illiterate masses.

Family

The position of the family in the Chinese traditional social structure provides a further example of diversity within a unified framework. The family was the prime collective unit to which all individual interests were secondary. Wealth was family wealth, and any individual's social prestige both stemmed from and reflected upon his family's standing in the community. Individualism, as understood in the West, was condemned as selfishness. The family training of the young sought to develop in them, not the ability "to stand on one's own two feet," but the social skills necessary to live harmoniously within the family, and, through it, within a society of similar families.

Families rather than individuals were the basic building blocks of the social, political, and economic structure. Thus choice of career or selection of a mate for marriage were not mainly matters of individual concern but were family affairs, subject, as were all fundamental questions, to the older generation's guiding authority.

Political and social practice reinforced these attitudes. All members of a family were held mutually responsible for the taxes, debts, and even the conduct of its members. You were, indeed, your brother's keeper. Litigation between family members was forbidden. Law codes reinforced the family's hierarchic structure—whatever the provocation, a son striking back at his father or a daughter-in-law retaliating against a mother-in-law were subject to severe punishments, as well as harsh social condemnation. On the other hand, full legal and social sanction justified the father's or mother-in-law's repressive or even physical chastisement of the younger generation. Escape was difficult, if not impossible. The return of a married daughter to her parents' home brought social shame as well as an economic burden. In a society where economic enterprises, and hence possibilities for employment, were family-based, the prospects for a runaway were bleak indeed.

The Chinese view of the family was much more all-encompassing than the modern western view. It was patrilineal, or based totally on the male line of descent. Women, upon marriage, were "lost" to the family of their birth and were thenceforth tied to the family of marriage, their inferior position emphasized by the absence of any rights of inheritance. The "family" included all deceased, all present, and all prospective members. A person saw himself as only a temporary holder and transmitter of a family heritage much greater in importance than any particular generation, not to mention any particular individual. The family provided the only social services available to the individual—financial security, social position, protection against outsiders, and even the assurance, in old age, of being honoured and supported by one's sons. A strong preference developed for burial in one's native place, where someone of the same name would remember one's deeds. With Neo-Confucianism's influence on social values in the last centuries of traditional Chinese society, filial piety became the most honoured social virtue, binding together families and generations past and present.

Within the accepted practice of "familyism," there was nevertheless considerable diversity. A peasant family's income expectations limited the size of the unit that could be supported to five or six people — more children would simply mean relying on the death of some members, or the sale of excess members into servitude, to ensure the family's survival through the frequent years of hunger or famine. Higher on the social ladder, the size of the average family increased dramatically. The living family spread out horizontally to incorporate a greater number of aunts and uncles; it also stretched out vertically, as the list of deceased relatives honoured in yearly ceremonies grew longer. In contrast, the simple ceremonies of the peasants honoured only the ancestors who had existed within the memory of its living members. Ancestor worship, like filial piety, was common to all levels of the society, but the form of its practice varied directly with one's economic status.

Further comment is perhaps necessary concerning the "gentry." Gentry families generally lived in local market towns or cities, rather than in the peasant villages. Being part of the gentry implied landownership, academic achievement, social position, and privilege. Although their income might be supplemented by holding official posts or investing quietly in local commerce, the gentry generally depended on agricultural wealth produced by tenant farmers or labourers. While a gentry "estate" only rarely reached the size of the average North American family farm, it was at this social level that one perceived the larger family unit with several married sons and their families remaining within the parental home.

The greater size of gentry families demanded greater discipline in inter-personal relations. On the death of the patriarch (the eldest male, who was head of the family), his unchallengeable authority passed on to his eldest son. However, all surviving sons had equal rights of inheritance to the family property. Splitting up the property could, within one or two generations, reduce the family estate to individual portions no larger than a rich peasant's holdings. It was obviously more practical to keep the family unit, and the estate, intact. However, to continue living together harmoniously (as was also society's ideal pattern) required obedience to formal rules of behaviour. In a peasant family, years of working closely together could result in a warm, easy-going relationship between father and son, with the latter having considerable influence on family decisions. In gentry families, with probably several sons (and grandsons) and therefore a more complex household environment, father-son relations tended to be formal and distant—even though expressed in proper Confucian terms of paternal concern and filial devotion. A far greater segregation of the sexes also distinguished gentry family life from the more relaxed relations among the peasantry. Peasant girls had almost constant opportunities in the village or in the fields for social contact with males outside the family circle. In contrast, a rich gentry family's daughter, from age five or six onward, received a separate upbringing from that of her brothers and male cousins, and had almost no contact with non-family males until the day she was sent to the home of a husband she might never have seen before.

The relationship between the gentry and the scholar-officials was particularly close. Most of the latter came from gentry families by virtue of their fathers' greater financial ability and social incentive to educate their sons. In the middle of the nineteenth century, it is estimated, 1.5 million holders of the lower degree constituted the base of the gentry class, in comparison to only 28 000 who went on to achieve upper-level degrees and bureaucratic postings. These figures indicate that the majority of degree-holders returned to their rural towns or small cities rather than becoming (or even planning to become) scholar-officials. At home, they were supported by the revenue of their family estates, receiving extra income from the various roles they assumed in local society — as arbitrators of disputes or as patrons of community enterprises such as maintenance of temples, management of the market, or organization of irrigation projects. They also acted as the community's line of communication with the imperial government's local representative. If a high bureaucratic family in the capital encountered imperial displeasure or a similar loss of prestige, it would "retire" to the rural seat of its landholding base. Thus, although examinations and government itself were city-centred, society's highest social class, the scholar-officials, retained strong roots in the countryside.

Before leaving this brief sketch of the traditional Chinese family and society, we should try to balance the picture of repression that has emerged thus far. Indeed, subordination was a key characteristic —subordination of the individual to the group, of youth to the older generation, of wife to husband. Many other features appear strange to western minds—marriages arranged as family rather than individual affairs, a stress on the production of offspring (particularly boys) rather than on loving relations between husband and wife, and, among the wealthy, the practice of concubinage, or "secondary wives" (usually for sexual gratification, but also for social prestige, and, if the first wife proved barren, for continuation of the family line). These customs should not be allowed to obscure the fact that family life in traditional China provided a warm, friendly environment. The Chinese love of children is legendary. Not to be married, if one could afford it, was unthinkable and not to have children and grandchildren was a catastrophe in emotional as well as economic terms. The family and the society were organized along status levels which had at least one distinct advantage—a person always had the security of knowing just where he stood within the family and the society. He knew that as long as he fulfilled the obligations pertaining to his status, he would receive the benefits of membership in his family and society. Always around him were other supportive members to share his problems and fate. What we may think of the traditional Chinese family system is less important, perhaps, than understanding that, in the eyes of the Chinese, it possessed very positive features and thus became a fundamental and lasting institution in their culture.

In examining the unity and diversity within traditional China, we can see that there were divisive forces. Regional diversities based on geography, language, and economics were reinforced by sharp differences in class wealth, expectations, and prestige. Nevertheless, cultural ideals and practices, perhaps even more than the political structure, provided effective counter-forces. Despite diversities, China remained, through centuries of history, a single, viable entity in the minds of its people.

Pottery tomb-guardian, T'ang period (left); sixteenth-century Ming porcelain plate (above).

This carving from a single block of ivory is contemporary evidence of continuing traditional craftsmanship.

Analysis

1. Was language a force of unity or disunity in China? Why? Some countries have more than one official language. Compare the experiences of one such country with that of China.

2. What would be the advantages and disadvantages from your point of view of being raised as a child in a Chinese family?

3. Compare the values and characteristics of the traditional Chinese family to those of your own.

4. How do the characteristics of the family unit reflect the underlying values of the whole society?

Suggested Readings

Ch'u T'ung-tzu, "Chinese Class Structure and Its Ideology," in J. K. Fairbank, ed., *Chinese Thought and Institutions* (Chicago: University of Chicago Press, 1957, 235-50).

Authoritative analysis of hierarchical social pattern of traditional China.

Fei Hsiao-t'ung, *China's Gentry: Essays on Rural-Urban Relations* (Chicago: University of Chicago Press, 1953).

Based on early-twentieth-century society, this work also covers the traditional gentry establishment, and contains six interesting family case studies.

O. Lang, *Chinese Family and Society* (New Haven, Conn.: Yale University Press, 1946.)

Covers both traditional and early modern periods.

Tsao Hsueh-chin, *Dream of the Red Chamber*, translated and adapted by C. C. Wang (Garden City, N.Y.: Doubleday Anchor Books, 1958).

A classic Chinese novel of an eighteenth-century, upper-gentry family, with excellent portrayal of attitudes and practices in the highest social levels.

SECTION I SUMMARY AND RESEARCH

1. Considering the geographical, cultural, economic, and philosophical diversity in China, was the emperor type of political system suitable for China at that time?

2. Why did the early dynasties have difficulty in establishing a unified state? Was this due to existing conditions, the weaknesses of the rulers, or poor political strategy?

3. Compare the Chinese élite with the élite in your country. Account for the differences.

4. Compare the thought of Mencius with John Locke's idea of sovereignty of the people and justification of revolution when rulers do not protect their "life, health, liberty, or possessions."

5. Study Chinese landscape painting. What does this type of art reflect about the Chinese view of the world and of humanity?

6. Trace the roots of the written Chinese language.

SECTION II
INITIAL ENCOUNTERS
WITH MODERNITY

Palaces of late Imperial China: the Summer Palace near Peking, rebuilt for the last Empress Dowager (upper); one of several courtyards and halls within the Forbidden City, home of emperors of the Ming and Ch'ing periods and now open to the public as a museum (lower).

CHAPTER 6
Early Modern China and the Outside World

Chronology

T'ang dynasty (618–906)
  819 Han Yü's petition to the Emperor against the Buddha bone

Sung dynasty (960–1279)

Yüan dynasty (1279–1368)   Mongol invasion
  Marco Polo (1254–1342) 1279–1292, in China; 1298, *Description of the World*
    dictated in Genoa Jail.

Ming dynasty (1368–1644)
  1514 arrival of first Portuguese in China
Matteo Ricci (1552-1610) 1582, arrival in China; 1601, permission to reside in
    Peking

Ch'ing dynasty (1644–1911)   Manchu invasion
  1692 Edict of Toleration of Christianity.
  1715 Papal Bull condemning Jesuit missionary practices in China
  1724 Chinese Emperor brands Christianity as heterodox sect.
  1793 edict of Emperor Ch'ien-lung rejecting the Macartney Mission's efforts to
    liberalize trade arrangements.

The Chinese had always sharply distinguished their own culture from
those of others. But from the fourteenth century onward they increasingly looked upon the world as clearly divided between ''inner'' and
''outer,'' Chinese and non-Chinese. Convinced that domestic stability
and order demanded the separation of the two and the isolation of the
''outer'' realm to prevent ''inner'' contamination, they regarded China

as possessing the sole culture deserving of the label "civilization." The name "China" was probably derived by outsiders from the name of the Ch'in dynasty; to the Chinese, their country was *Chung-kuo*, the Middle Kingdom, located at the centre of the world and surrounded by lesser realms. Just as the Chinese regarded as natural the inequalities of status within family and society, so also they ranked these outer peoples and cultures in a "natural" hierarchy determined by their greater or lesser accord with the uniqueness and superiority of China's own civilization. Threats to security and even invasion by "outer barbarians" were expected, but the Chinese believed that history demonstrated that renewed dedication to traditional practices and values was their best protection. The Chinese accepted the truth of the ancient Confucian saying, "When there is internal disorder, external disasters will occur."

From the early days of the Chou dynasty, Chinese foreign policy had focussed on protecting the wealth and agriculture of China from the warlike, nomadic tribes to the north and west. The Chinese attitude to these barbarians may be summed up in the words attributed to Mencius: "I have heard of barbarians being transformed by Chinese ways, but I have never heard of China being transformed by the barbarians."[14] This superior attitude to foreigners evolved from centuries of contact not only with nomadic tribal peoples but also with Koreans, Japanese, Southeast Asians, Arabs, and others, and it was automatically extended to Europeans when they appeared in the Far East.

The Concept of "Barbarians"

In the early ninth century, a strait-laced Confucian scholar named Han Yü (768–824) addressed a memorial to the reigning emperor, denouncing a proposed grand festival welcoming the purported fingerbone of Buddha into the capital city. Han Yü's arguments represented the classic views of agnostic Confucianism:

> Now Buddha was a man of the barbarians who did not speak the language of China and wore clothes of a different fashion. His sayings did not

concern the ways of our ancient kings, nor did his manner of dress conform to their laws. . . . If he were still alive today and came to our court by order of his ruler, Your Majesty might condescend to receive him, but it would amount to no more than one audience in the Hsüan-cheng Hall, a banquet by the Office for Receiving Guests, the presentation of a suit of clothes, and he would then be escorted to the borders of the nation, dismissed, and not allowed to delude the masses.[15]

This sense of the eternal superiority of all things Chinese was very much in contrast to the prevailing spirit of Han Yü's times, for the T'ang dynasty stands out in Chinese history as the most confident, rich, and cosmopolitan in tastes. In fact, Han Yü's protest coincided with the Golden Age of Buddhism in Chinese society, and it resulted in his near execution and banishment by an unsympathetic and devout emperor.

Later Chinese historians criticized the cosmopolitanism of the T'ang culture as being partly responsible for that dynasty's decline and eventual collapse. The succeeding Sung dynasty, for all its philosophic and cultural splendour, was also militarily weak, and eventually it succumbed to the onslaught of a small number of vigorous Mongols led by Kublai Khan. In the long history of foreign threats to Chinese culture, the Mongols' Yüan dynasty was regarded by later Chinese as the most "barbaric" and the least sensitive to traditional Chinese practices and norms. Its fate illustrated the depth of Chinese feeling about such insensitivity: after less than a century, the Mongols were thrown out by the Ming dynasty, a Chinese ruling house, which set out to cleanse the "inner" realm of contamination from the years of "outer" influence. As part of this "renativization," Neo-Confucianism—the branch of Confucian thought which considered Han Yü as one of its early contributors—was formally recognized as the basic orthodoxy of the examination and educational systems.

The Ming dynasty lasted nearly three centuries. During its final decades, corrupt politics, and a growing administrative ineptness in coping with deteriorating economic conditions, touched off massive peasant rebellions which toppled the native royal house but allowed an alien people, the Manchus, to seize imperial power. One might expect this foreign Ch'ing dynasty (1644–1911) to run counter to the Chinese sense of cultural superiority. Indeed, many Chinese scholar-officials, loyal to the memory of the defeated Ming, resisted the Manchu conquest on precisely the grounds of its foreign origins. But the Manchu rulers, while careful to insulate their small numbers by special privileged status, nevertheless conscientiously sought acceptance from the Chinese by championing time-honoured Chinese values. Government structures and practices remained essentially the same, and Neo-Confucian texts were reaffirmed as the orthodox subject matter for all education and examinations. The government also sponsored grand projects to compile literary and artistic works, and thereby gave remunerative employment to many Chinese scholars. Emphasizing the cultural rather than the racial or national base of Chinese self-definition, the Manchu rulers carefully built up the case for their legitimacy.

The best illustration of the non-Chinese dynasty's championing of Chinese culturalism is found in a statement of the late-eighteenth-century Emperor Ch'ien-lung to George III of England. In 1793 England had sent an embassy under Lord Macartney to seek better trade relations and diplomatic contacts. The Emperor's edict in response to these requests was given in the tone not of a foreign Manchu overlord, but of a Chinese "Son of Heaven":

> You, O King, are so inclined toward our civilization that you have sent a special envoy across the seas to bring to our Court your memorial of congratulations on the occasion of my birthday and to present your native products as an expression of your thoughtfulness. On perusing your memorial, so simply worded and sincerely conceived, I am impressed by your genuine respectfulness and friendliness and am greatly pleased.

(And, after rejecting the English requests to station an ambassador in Peking and to include China in the world of European international trade and political relations, the Emperor concluded:)

> The Celestial Court has pacified and possessed the territory within the four seas. Its sole aim is to do its utmost to achieve good government and to manage political affairs, attaching no value to strange jewels and precious objects. The various articles presented by you, O King, this time are

accepted by my special order to the office in charge of such functions in consideration of the offerings having come from a long distance with sincere good wishes. As a matter of fact, the virtue and prestige of the Celestial Dynasty having spread far and wide, the kings of the myriad nations come by land and sea with all sorts of precious things. Consequently there is nothing we lack, as your principal envoy and others have themselves observed. We have never set much store on strange or ingenious objects, nor do we need any more of your country's manufactures. . . .[16]

Trade with other nations was not considered an economic necessity for China, but was rather a favour by the compassionate Chinese Emperor to the unfortunates of the world who were not Chinese. No native son on the Middle Kingdom's Dragon Throne could have more eloquently expressed the spirit of Chinese culturalism.

The Barbarian's China

The West of the late eighteenth century, however, was not an outlying nomadic culture, and Britain in particular did not feel itself inferior to other countries—to, for example, Korea or Annam, which the Chinese ranked higher than the West because they had borrowed heavily from the Chinese civilization. For several centuries, the West had had token contact with China, and both traders and missionaries had brought back extraordinary tales of life inside the Middle Kingdom. But the West was now less willing to accept China's isolation or its sense of its own superiority.

The most famous of early western travellers to China was Marco Polo, the intrepid Venetian adventurer of the late thirteenth century. A keen observer, he travelled extensively in China and actually served for a time as a minor official for the Mongol conquerors. His accounts of the country, dictated while in jail after his return to Italy, were flavoured by his gift for exaggeration, but their essential accuracy provided the West with a portrait of a rich, highly cultured, and orderly society. However, except for Marco Polo's corroboration of western rumours of fabulous wealth in the East, his accounts were dismissed by contemporaries as too fanciful. Rediscovering the glories of its own past and building a new society, late-medieval and early-Renaissance

Europe could not accept Polo's vision of a highly developed civilization outside the Christian world.

Polo's essential accuracy was only substantiated centuries later by the reports of Jesuit missionaries who sought to spread the Catholic faith in the wake of Portuguese and Spanish commercial and colonial expansion into Asia. The Italian Jesuit, Matteo Ricci, reached the Portuguese outpost of Macao, on China's southeastern coastline, in 1582 and began his efforts to establish a permanent Christian mission within China proper. Some nineteen years later he was permitted to reside in the capital, Peking. His burial there in 1610 included imperial honours, a mark of the respect he had won from the Chinese court. Over the succeeding century, a handful of Jesuits and missionaries from other orders made possible a fascinating period of East-West contacts.

Like Ricci himself, the later Jesuit missionaries were highly educated in Renaissance sciences as well as in Christian theology, and they generally followed Ricci's pattern of deliberate self-adaptation to the China scene. Learning the language, dressing in the Chinese manner, becoming knowledgeable in the rich classical heritage of their hosts, these missionaries also made themselves useful as scientists, mathematicians, translators, and surveyors in the imperial courts of both late Ming and early Ch'ing times. In 1692, in recognition of their secular services, the reigning emperor granted an official edict of toleration for the propagation and practice of the Catholic faith. Ricci's dream of a mutually respectful meeting between East and West seemed close to fruition.

However, the early eighteenth century saw the end of such tolerance. From the European side, the Pope, in 1715, condemned the Jesuit accommodations to Chinese beliefs and practices. For example, he specifically denounced the Jesuit interpretation of the annual Chinese festivals and ceremonies connected with ancestor worship. Ricci and his successors had viewed these in the Confucian secular manner, as civil rather than religious rites and hence perfectly compatible with conversion to Christianity. The hostile stand of Rome insisted on Chinese converts dissociating themselves from all non-Christian rites honouring ancestors. The Chinese Emperor could not tolerate such external interference with practices so important to social unity within China. His reply to the papal declaration was an edict expelling any missionary who departed from these Jesuit accommodations. In 1724 Christianity was publicly declared an unacceptable, or heterodox, sect. Although Jesuits remained at court throughout the eighteenth century in positions connected with their secular expertise, their religious mission was fatally damaged.

By the end of the eighteenth century, sporadic government persecutions and virulent attacks by the Confucian scholar-gentry had wiped out all but vestiges of Christianity within China. Henceforth, the Chinese looked upon western missionaries and their religious message as subversive of traditional Chinese values. Westerners were also under suspicion as possible agents of external interference in Chinese domestic affairs. This growing distrust resulted in the burial, in forgotten Chinese archives, of numerous translations and writings by Jesuit missionaries and Chinese converts on the subject of western secular knowledge. Thus, a fruitful phase of cultural interaction between China and the West came to an end, with Chinese cultural isolation reasserted in even fuller strength.

Meanwhile, Jesuit letters and reports on China had a quite different reception than Marco Polo's earlier descriptions. They startled Europe with the image of a wealthy, highly developed, non-Christian civilization, harbouring a rich and independent tradition in the arts and sciences. Reinforced by growing trade connections, these Jesuit portraits touched off popular enthusiasm for exotic Chinese artifacts, particularly in England, France, and the German states. In painting, landscape gardening, architecture, ceramics, and the decorative arts, mid-eighteenth-century Europe indulged itself in imagined Chinese tastes. This wave of *chinoiserie*, as it was called, resulted in the establishment of a whole new industry in south China, producing "Chinese" goods on order for European markets, though the products would never have met the aesthetic tastes of China's own native markets.

On reading the reports of the Jesuits, some Europeans envied China.

Critical of their own society, they imagined China to be the ideal state. As one European intellectual wrote in 1769:

China offers an enchanting picture of what the whole world might become, if the laws of that empire were to become the laws of all nations. Go to Peking! Gaze upon the mightiest of mortals; he is the true and perfect image of Heaven![17]

To European philosophers of the Enlightenment, who tried to break down traditional western patterns of religious authority in the church and rule by Divine Right in the state, China provided concrete evidence for the virtues of a secularized morality, a rational "enlightened despotism" serving the people's welfare, and a government by a scholarly élite rather than by a hereditary aristocracy. In 1764 Voltaire, one of the most ardent mid-eighteenth-century users of the Jesuits' reports, stated: "One need not be obsessed with the merits of the Chinese to recognize at least that the organization of their empire is in truth the best that the world has ever seen. . . . "[18]

The artistic craze for chinoiserie and the Enlightenment's rosy picture of China were relatively short-lived. In 1824, sixty years after Voltaire's enthusiastic statement, Ralph Waldo Emerson equally succinctly expressed the changed western image:

The closer contemplation we condescend to bestow, the more disgustful is that booby nation. The Chinese Empire enjoys precisely a Mummy's reputation, that of having preserved to a hair for 3 or 4,000 years the ugliest features in the world. I have no gift to see a meaning in the venerable vegetation of this extraordinary (nation) people. They are tools for other nations to use. Even miserable Africa can say I have hewn the wood and drawn the water to promote the civilization of other lands. But China, reverent dullness! hoary ideot [sic]!, all she can say at the convocation of nations must be — "I made the tea."[19]

China, unknowingly on its own part, and without any fundamental change in its own state of affairs, was no longer considered a model for western countries to emulate.

Between Voltaire and Emerson, Europe underwent vast political, social, and economic changes, marked by the upheavals of the French Revolution and the beginning of the Industrial Revolution. The new westerners who sought to open the doors into China were not Renaissance intellectuals, accommodating priests, or enlightened philosophers; they were ambitious traders seeking riches and determined missionaries looking for souls to convert. Close behind came the colonial administrators, ready to rule and organize the world. These new westerners were much less impressed by China's grand tradition, stretching back thousands of years. Unlike the West, China could not boast of foreign voyages of discovery, steam engines and factories, modern weapons, and popular institutions.

China's refusal to recognize that the shoe of cultural superiority was now on the other foot increasingly frustrated western apostles of progress. A mid-nineteenth-century popular British magazine ditty illustrated those new racist sentiments:

*A Chanson for Canton**

JOHN CHINAMAN a rogue is born,
The laws of truth he holds in scorn;
About as great a brute as can
Encumber the Earth is JOHN CHINAMAN.
  Sing Yeh, my cruel JOHN CHINAMAN,
  Sing Yeo, my stubborn JOHN CHINAMAN;
  Not COBDEN† himself can take off the ban
  By humanity laid on JOHN CHINAMAN.[20]

* Only Chinese port open to foreigners after 1760
† Noted nineteenth-century British liberal

Convinced of the importance of trade and diplomatic intercourse between nations, and accepting without question his own social practices as the marks of civilized behaviour, the westerner took a low view of Chinese customs without taking the trouble to understand them.

The Chinese, on their part, returned the favour, as we see in the following Chinese description of a western dinner party in 1831:

Judge now what tastes people possess who sit at table and swallow bowls of a fluid, in their outlandish tongue called *Soo-pe*, and next devour the flesh of fish, served in a manner as near as may be to resemble the living fish itself. Dishes of half-raw meat are then placed at various angles of the table;

these float in gravy, while from them pieces are cut with sword-like instruments and placed before the guests. Really it was not until I beheld this sight that I became convinced of what I had often heard, that the ferocious disposition of these demons arises from their indulgence in such gross food. . . . Then a green and white substance, the smell of which was overpowering. This I was informed was a compound of sour buffalo milk, baked in the sun, under whose influence it is allowed to remain until it becomes filled with insects, yet, the greener and more lively it is, with the more relish is it eaten. This is called *Che-Sze*, and is accompanied by the drinking of a muddy red fluid which foams up over the tops of the drinking cups, soils one's clothes, and is named *Pe-Urh*—think of that! *When* will these uncivilized men become versed in the precepts of the gastronomist whom I have named, and make offerings of red candles and gilt paper on altars raised to his memory?[21]

West and East viewed each other's habits with a wry amusement at best, while dress and social mannerisms remained the topics of numerous derogatory jokes on both sides. In short, in the early part of the nineteenth century, the Chinese considered western countries, in their bewildering strangeness, as unequal to even Siam or Korea, while the westerners saw in Chinese agrarianism and exclusiveness the very marks of inferiority.

Analysis

1. Explain how China justified the view that the outside world was "barbaric" compared to her civilization. Select any other country at the same period of time as a comparison.

2. Account for the different attitudes toward China expressed by Voltaire and Emerson (p. 74).

3. What factors have influenced your country's attitude toward China since 1949?

4. Conduct an objectively worded survey in your class or community in order to discover present-day attitudes toward China. Analyse your results.

5. Discuss the case for and against the Jesuit missionaries in China.

Suggested Readings

R. Dawson, *The Chinese Chameleon: An Analysis of European Conceptions of Chinese Civilization* (London: Oxford University Press, 1967).
Good general history of western perspectives on China, complete with interesting illustrations.

C. P. Fitzgerald, *The Chinese View of their Place in the World* (London: Oxford University Press, 1964).
An excellent short summary of China's attitudes toward foreign relations and foreigners, it covers both traditional and modern times.

Wolfgang Franke, *China and the West: The Cultural Encounter, 13th to 20th Centuries* (New York: Harper Torchbooks, 1967).
A general historical treatment of the history of Chinese foreign relations in the early modern and modern periods.

J. Spence, *The China Helpers: Western Advisers in China, 1620–1960* (London: The Bodley Head, 1969).
Chapter I, "To God Through the Stars," is a succinct account of the Jesuit mission in seventeenth-century China.

CHAPTER 7
Century of Shame: The Outer Realm

Chronology
1760 Canton system of foreign trade begins.
1796 China's ban on import or production of opium; imports, however, continue, averaging c. 4500 chests (almost 60 kg each) yearly import, 1800–21.
1838 Opium imports reach c. 40000 chests.
1839 March 10, Lin Tse-hsü (1785–1850) arrives at Canton as Imperial Commissioner charged with ending opium trade.
     November, first naval battle of Opium War with Britain.
1842 August 29, Treaty of Nanking initiating new era of Treaty Settlements (French, Americans, and others conclude similar treaties in next two years).
1854 Organization of nucleus which in 1863 becomes Shanghai International Settlement and French Concession.
1858 Outbreak of second Anglo-Chinese ("Arrow") War, resulting in Treaties of Tientsin, which, following difficulties in exchange of ratifications in 1859, lead to renewed conflict.
1860 Anglo-French forces occupy Peking and force new Convention.
1861 Creation at Peking of Tsungli-yamen, an office to handle foreign relations.
1870 Tientsin anti-Christian riot ends Co-operative Policy and inaugurates era of "gunboat diplomacy".
1877 First permanent Chinese embassy abroad in Britain.
1879 Opium imports, legalized under 1858–60 treaties, peak at 87000 chests, declining thereafter due to domestic production.
1883-5 Sino-French war over Annam's status.
1886 China forced to acknowledge British protectorate in Burma.
1894-5 Sino-Japanese War.

The nineteenth century was a traumatic period of challenge to cherished institutions around the globe. In the West, urban mass movements and democratic institutions threatened and sometimes overwhelmed aristocratic and traditional systems. The spread of industrialization brought with it vast riches and power to those nations who participated in the new technology. New social classes, particularly the urban workers, or proletariat, multiplied in number, straining the society's old comfortable ways and values. Age-old beliefs and religious traditions were challenged by the spread of science and the beginnings of mass education.

Throughout the world, the dynamism of western nations experiencing these transformations found outlets in imperial ventures, exploitation of broken peoples, and the extension of western control and rule into large parts of the globe. As part of this process, the West would not allow China (or any other country) the right to non-participation in the new global network that was being created. China was forced into confrontation with the West, and also, as a by-product, into confrontation with its own past. For traditional China, the immediate consequences were humiliating and disastrous.

The New Barbarians

In the late eighteenth century, mounting European demands for tea, silk, and other Chinese products kept British traders busy; but these merchants were frustrated in their search for comparable products to balance their trade with China. Chinese self-sufficiency forced western traders to bring in large amounts of silver bullion in payment for their growing export of Chinese goods. Just at the end of the century, however, western traders found such a product in opium, which was produced mainly in British India and exported to China in growing amounts, despite Chinese prohibitions. The British East India Company both controlled opium production in India and held a monopoly on British trade with China. Officially, however, the company avoided direct contamination by this drug trade. They allowed private traders to buy the opium in India and to handle all the shipping and sale of the drug in China. In order to avoid Chinese customs vigilance at Canton—since 1760 the only port opened to western trade—foreign ships dropped off opium on western "receiving ships" anchored in the outer reaches of the Pearl River leading to Canton. With the connivance of corrupt Chinese local officials, Chinese middlemen spread the opium from the receiving ships through a radiating network in China. On board the private foreign trading-vessels, the westerners' superior seamanship and naval firepower protected their heavy investments from any threats by the ponderous war-junks and the outdated weaponry of Chinese naval patrols, as well as the coastal pirate fleets common to the area. The triangular trade between Britain, India, and China finally balanced the East India Company's ledger-books, as the opium trade reversed the flow of silver bullion.

The serious economic and social effects of opium addiction finally forced the Chinese court to take decisive action. In 1839 the Emperor dispatched Imperial Commissioner Lin Tse-hsü to destroy the forbidden trade. Severe measures against native addicts, pushers, and involved officials had already begun to neutralize the Chinese distribution network before Lin's arrival in Canton. Foreign traders responded by searching the coastline north of Canton for new smuggling outlets. Lin decided that to eradicate the native trade it was also necessary to strike at its source, namely the western importers.

Lin's subsequent actions were typical of traditional Chinese political practice, combining high moral purpose and authoritarian administrative action. In late March 1839, he applied the Chinese principle of the community's responsibility for the illegal actions of individuals. On his orders, Chinese soldiers effectively bottled up the foreign community in Canton, without servants or supplies, until the British Trade Commissioner undertook to deliver the entire stock of opium held by the illicit receiving ships. Much to the surprise of cynics within the British merchant community, Lin actually destroyed the 20 000-odd surrendered chests.

In July, open conflict came closer. A Chinese died during a drunken brawl with British sailors, and the strict Chinese laws on homicide required a culprit. However, the British insisted that they could not discover the actual murderer and refused to hand over a stand-in for Chinese justice. In effect, they refused to admit the right of Chinese criminal jurisdiction over British subjects. At this point, Lin replied by

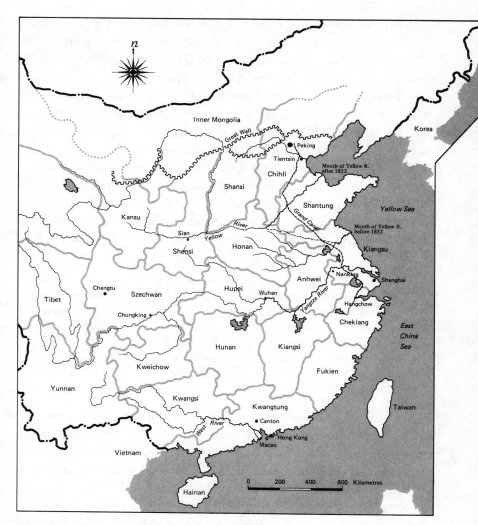

Map 5   Administrative Areas under the Ch'ing Dynasty

cutting off all British trade. Confident of its military power and legal correctness, Britain resorted to war, ostensibly over the high-handed manner of Lin's actions against the foreign community. All other nations trading with China sat back to await the final outcome.

Britain's military might quickly overwhelmed the Chinese forces, which had experienced long years of peace, administrative laxity, and official corruption. A maximum of 10 000 British troops encountered only minor setbacks in three summer campaigns up the southeast coastline and into the lower Yangtze valley. At Nanking in mid-1842 the Chinese sued for peace, as it became clear that the once-proud military might of the Manchu dynasty had proved unable to check the rapid advance of the small British attacking force.

In keeping with its stand that war arose over lofty issues of principle—free trade, individual rights, and diplomatic proprieties—Britain omitted the opium question from the negotiated peace. In a later reminiscence, however, an old-time employee of the British East India Company in pre-1842 Canton gave a more cynical view of events:

> The Chinese had not looked with satisfaction upon the concessions they had been obliged to make to an overwhelming military and naval force, which had caused them the loss of myriads of lives, often under circumstances of great atrocity, of unheard-of suffering, as well as many millions of dollars independently of the war indemnity. The ordeal was a terrible one; but they gained by it the, to them, unenvied *privilege* of falling in with Western ideas. . . . With the sword at their throat they have become members of what is facetiously called the "Brotherhood" of Nations![22]

A more typical contemporary opinion, perhaps, was that expressed by the British Foreign Minister, Lord Palmerston: "There is no doubt that this event, which will form an epoch in the progress of the civilization of the human races, must be attended with most important advantages to the commercial interests of England."[23] Unfortunately for both sides, the treaty settlement of 1842 marked only a temporary respite in the application of force as a response to frustrations created by mutual misunderstanding and clashing values.

The Opium War was just the first of a series of humiliating experiences for China at the hands of Britain and other western nations. By the end of the nineteenth century, four more major clashes occurred—in 1858–60 with Britain and France, in 1883–5 with France, in 1894–5 with Japan, and in 1899–1900 with all western powers joined by Japan—as well as minor incidents. Each defeat resulted in Chinese territorial concessions to the colonial forces. The island of Hong Kong became a British colony in 1842, and the adjoining Kowloon peninsula was added in 1860. In 1880 Japan, without challenge, occupied the Liuchiu (Ryūkyū) Islands claimed by both countries, and in 1885 France forced China to renounce its traditional suzerainty in the emerging French protectorate of Annam. To avoid being outflanked by the growing French Empire in Indo-China, Britain, a year later, forced a similar Chinese recognition of British protectorate rights in Burma, another border country which traditionally rendered tributary homage to Peking in recognition of China's vague suzerain rights. Japan's victory in 1895 gained Taiwan and the Pescadores Islands for the Japanese Empire, and China was further forced to renounce claims of suzerainty over Korea. It seemed that only China's large size and immense population, plus the western rivalries among the colonial powers themselves, prevented any one power from aspiring to a complete takeover.

The Treaty Format

The western presence in China in the nineteenth and early twentieth centuries was governed by what came to be called the "unequal treaty" system, a collective term for various international agreements forced upon the Chinese after each confrontation with western military power. Besides the territorial concessions already mentioned, these treaties refashioned Chinese-western relations in a number of important ways:

1. Western Diplomatic and Commercial Contact

The first treaties of the 1840s contained clauses demanding respectful treatment for western diplomatic personnel and their rights to open communication on an equal basis with corresponding officials in the Chinese bureaucracy. This fundamentally challenged traditional Chinese practices, which were based on a concept of the "natural" hierarchy of nations and refused to concede the equality of foreign and Chinese officials. The Chinese initially avoided the issue. For example, in response to pressure for a discussion of treaty revision by

British, French, and American representatives in 1853–4, both the Canton and the Shanghai governors-general sent word that they did not think any talks were necessary and that they lacked authority from the Chinese court to engage in such discussions. When the foreign diplomats subsequently visited Tientsin, Chinese court officials turned them back, saying that only those same southern officials had the responsibility for foreign relations. These tactics led to British demands in the 1860 treaties for permanently stationed diplomatic representatives in the Chinese capital. This normal European practice was fundamentally opposite to Chinese tradition, and British insistence on this arrangement represented another serious loss of prestige for the reigning dynasty.

China reluctantly established its own foreign embassies only in the late 1870s. The traditional idea of cultural contamination by intimacy with the "barbarians" tenaciously persisted. China's "entry into the family of nations," by force and in a distinctly inferior position in a world-wide order of nations, contrasted sharply with its former free and superior position at the apex of the Asian hierarchy.

A similar fate befell China's traditional tight controls over foreign trade. Prior to 1840, only Canton was open to foreign traders, and the Chinese had set up controls to limit foreign influence. No foreign women were allowed upriver from Macao to Canton, for instance. Foreign traders could reside only in the "Factory Quarter" of Canton, and only during the trading season, after which they had to retire to isolated Macao or overseas. A limited number of designated Chinese, known as the "hong merchants," exercised the government monopoly on foreign trade. The hong merchants assumed responsibility for the foreigners' conduct and handled all their communications with Chinese officials. While the official customs duties on trade were low, a bewildering and quite arbitrary mosaic of supplementary fees and bribes frustrated the foreigners. By means of these "extras," local officials prospered, though their social status as Confucian bureaucrats denied them direct participation in trade.

The treaties of the 1840s swept aside this "Canton system" in favour of open trade and permanent foreign residence in Canton and

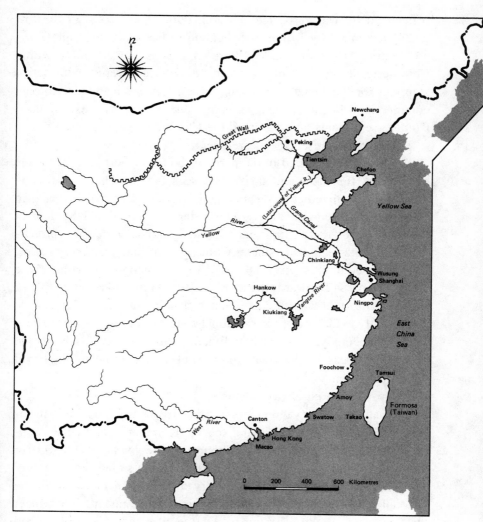

Map 6   The Early Treaty Ports, 1842–74

four additional treaty ports farther up the southeast coastline. Subsequent arrangements added to the number of treaty ports and opened up northern and interior regions for penetration by western traders and missionaries. From the first treaties, China's right to control its own official tariffs was restricted. Custom duties were fixed at the low levels demanded by Britain's dedication to free-trade principles, and all "extras" were eliminated. Foreign vessels moved freely within Chinese territorial and inland waters, directly competing with native shipping for the lucrative carrying trade. The application of foreign commercial principles, whatever their value in western eyes, offended Chinese sentiments and disrupted the Chinese economic system.

2. Privileged Presence of Foreigners

The foreigners resided in the parts of the treaty port cities set aside exclusively for them and their Chinese servants. Their concession areas were set up either as separated units for different nations or, as in Shanghai, as a co-operatively administered International Settlement (although, even there, the French insisted on a separate French quarter). Although technically under Chinese territorial suzerainty, in effect Chinese administrative authority was not recognized within these areas. From 1842 onward, the treaties also established the principle of "extra-territoriality," which stipulated that foreigners in China were subject only to the law of their national consular representatives. These rights were enjoyed by each individual foreigner, not only in the concession areas of the treaty ports, but wherever he might travel within the country.

3. Most-Favoured-Nation Status

International trade agreements today frequently contain "most-favoured-nation" clauses, giving special treatment to particular countries. Such agreements between countries are made selectively, to serve the mutual advantage of both parties. China's nineteenth-century experience with this practice was very different. Included in all the unequal treaties, the most-favoured-nation clause meant, in essence, that any new "rights" wrung by one country out of the weakened Chinese state were automatically conferred on all others. Thus the United States, by including this clause in its 1844 treaty with China, acquired all the privileges subsequently secured by other countries, although the United States itself did not participate in armed conflict with China until 1900. Without gaining any advantages from this clause, China quickly found that it could not continue playing off one western power against another in self-protection.

4. Indemnities

In the West, the payment of indemnities by the losing side in the war was a common practice. In nineteenth-century China, victorious western powers applied this penalty with devastating psychological as well as economic effects. Besides the humiliation of defeat, the Chinese had to pay large amounts after each major confrontation. For example, among the penalties imposed by the peace treaty of 1895 that ended China's war with Japan was the payment of 200 million taels (a Chinese silver monetary unit) to the victor. When Russian, French, and German pressure forced Japan to return to China the Liaotung Peninsula in Manchuria (ceded to Japan in the peace agreement of 1895), China was forced to add another 30 million taels to the original indemnity. For comparison, the Manchu government's total annual revenue at this time was only 89 million taels.

Besides indemnities forced on China after major wars, other smaller sums were extracted following minor incidents, often in connection with local Chinese attacks on missionaries or other foreigners within the interior. This was particularly true after 1870 when "gunboat diplomacy" became a normal western practice. On hearing of an incident involving Chinese and westerners, the foreign consuls would rapidly dispatch gunboats to the scene before negotiations began on the terms of compensation for real and imagined damages to western property and prestige. The presence of gunboats, waiting to attack, put the Chinese negotiators at a serious disadvantage in the resultant talks.

Forced into the new "game" of international relations under foreign rules, China clung to the hope that interaction with foreigners was only temporary. The western powers held no such expectations. Lack of understanding on both sides continued to arouse mutual irritation. One modern writer has described the frustration of the foreigners:

In 1861, under constant prodding from the Western ambassadors, the Chinese established the Tsungli Yamen for the management of foreign affairs. Since the new office lacked traditional status and had to deal with unpleasant matters, it was initially staffed by officers who seemed to the foreigners to be peculiarly incompetent. There was a suspicion that the

Chinese had designed a clever stratagem for dealing with foreign officials—forcing them to conduct their business with the most dim-witted officials in all the empire. Many Western officials were nearly driven out of their minds. The tactics ranged from a persistent tendency of officials to "forget" all that had been agreed to at previous meetings, to the practice of confusing and mixing up the policy demands and interests of the various foreign powers.[24]

China gradually discovered that the problems it faced in foreign relations were not temporary, and that such tactics did not solve these difficulties. But while the foreigners could deal with their frustrations by exercising military might, the Chinese were not in any position to respond in kind.

In the face of humiliation and progressive western encroachment, the Chinese response was, indeed, slow to crystallize. The traditional political and economic system proved incapable of coping with internal disintegration, which was hastened, though by no means solely caused, by foreign intrusion. The time-honoured Confucian outlook, which stressed peace within the "inner" realm, initially blinded most Chinese to the implications of the new western presence. Only gradually, as this "outer" menace became intertwined with "inner" disturbances and the breakdown of society, did the Chinese begin to understand and to give serious consideration to the complex problems facing them.

Analysis

1. Draw up arguments from a British point of view to justify English policies in China during the nineteenth century. Criticize each argument from a Chinese point of view.

2. The lack of effective resistance by China to foreign imperialism in the nineteenth century was a result of its own decadence. Discuss the validity of this statement by referring to measures that China might have taken in order to resist the intrusion of foreign powers.

3. Discuss the underlying attitudes and strategies of China and Britain which brought about the Opium War. Judging only from the context of that historical

period, is it possible to place blame more on one side than another? Justify your answer.

Suggested Readings

Hu Sheng, *Imperialism and Chinese Politics:* 1840–1925 (Peking: Foreign Language Press, 1955). (Hardcover)

A good general introduction to the Marxist interpretation of western imperialism in China.

J. Spence, *The China Helpers: Western Advisers in China, 1620–1960* (London: The Bodley Head, 1969).

Chapters 2 through 5 trace careers in China of several types of westerners during the nineteenth century.

S. Y. Teng and J. K. Fairbank, eds., *China's Response to the West: A Documentary Survey, 1839–1923* (Cambridge: Harvard University Press, 1954).

Extensive coverage by translated documents, connected by explanatory comments.

A. Waley, *The Opium War Through Chinese Eyes* (London: Allen & Unwin, 1958).

A collection of Chinese materials from diaries, reports, etc., with special reference to Lin Tse-hsü, highly readable and illustrative of Chinese reactions to the events of the period.

CHAPTER 8
Century of Shame: The Inner Realm

Chronology

1796–1804 White Lotus Rebellion in middle Yangtze region.

1836 Hung Hsiu-ch'üan's (1814–64) first reading of Christian tracts.

1850 First clash of Hung's "God Worshippers Society" with imperial troops.

1851 Hung declares the Heavenly Kingdom of Great Peace (T'ai-p'ing t'ien-kuo).

1853 Taiping Rebellion establishes Nanking as capital; Nien rebellion in north China breaks out.

1854 Miao tribesmen in southwest rise in revolt.

1855 Chinese Moslems in southwest rise in revolt.

1860–1 Death of Emperor and enthronement of a minor under regency dominated by mother, Empress Dowager Tz'u-hsi (1835–1908).

1862 Moslems in northwest revolt; last surge of Taiping toward Shanghai turned back by Anhwei Army of Li Hung-chang (1823–1901), aided by "Ever Victorious Army" of foreign-trained Chinese under American Frederick Townsend Ward and, later, British Major George Gordon.

1864 Nanking recaptured by imperial troops and Taiping collapse.

1868 Li Hung-chang's Nien Army crushes Nien Rebellion.

1870 Li Hung-chang becomes governor-general at Tientsin.

1874 Moslem rebellions in southwest and northwest suppressed.

1875 Death of T'ung-chih Emperor and enthronement of four-year-old Kuang-hsü (r. 1875–1908) under regency of Empress Dowager Tz'u-hsi, his aunt.

1889 "Retirement" of Empress Dowager as Emperor reaches age of majority.

Traditional Chinese historians, steeped in Confucian principles, would have viewed the prospects of the Manchu dynasty at the beginning of the nineteenth century with some scepticism. Imbued with the classical view of history as a series of dynastic cycles following one another, they might have concluded that the evident prosperity, domestic order, and external security of this period marked a high point in the curve of the dynasty's ascendancy. They would have noted, however, that beneath these favourable conditions were signs of administrative negligence, a growing taste for luxury, and a neglect of one's duties. They might also have pointed to evidence of mushrooming corruption among the élite. In the Confucian view of history, such disintegration would inevitably engender discontent among the peasant masses, and eventually would cause riots and revolt. These, in turn, could only result in further internal disintegration or foreign invasion, unless checked by a return to austere Confucian moral values which would revitalize society. The threatened dynasty could either set its bureaucratic house in order or lose its mandate. Although early-nineteenth-century Manchu rule made such an assessment too dangerous to utter openly, the truth and logic of this traditional psychology seemed evident in the first signs of peasant unrest and the appearance of a small minority of reform-minded scholar-officials.

Rebellion

The first warning of new upheavals came at the turn of the century. A secret organization known as the White Lotus Society helped organize a widespread rebellion by dissatisfied peasantry. Eight long years of fighting between 1796 and 1804 pointed out both the extent of popular discontent and the woeful state of the dynasty's once-proud military system. Crushed eventually by government troops, the rebellion collapsed, although the White Lotus Society simply went underground and participated in several later rebellions.

As it turned out, the White Lotus uprising merely prefaced a new major upsurge of peasant-based discontent. Beginning in 1851, the dynasty faced a sequence of uncoordinated rebellions. Their common causes included the peasantry's economic desperation and a latent hostility toward the foreign dynasty that was no longer able to keep its house in order. Several rebellions also stemmed from the traditional resentment among ethnic minorities against the Han, or Chinese, majority, as government maladministration and economic depression combined to increase Chinese pressure on the minorities' semi-independence. When the British invasion of 1839–42 exposed the Manchus' military weakness, secret societies multiplied throughout the country. Government officials rightly feared these tightly knit brotherhoods as serious threats. The mid-nineteenth-century series of rebellions underlined the critical state of domestic affairs: the Taiping uprising in the south and central provinces; the Nien "bandits" (a traditional official label for any rebels) in the northeast; and the uprisings of both Moslem religious groups and Miao tribal groups in the northwest and southwest.

The Taiping uprising stemmed originally from peasant discontent in the southern provinces. The economic prosperity of the eighteenth century waned as population growth outstripped agricultural production. On the southeast coastline, swelling numbers of people left their homeland to seek fortunes abroad, considerably augmenting earlier, smaller Chinese communities in many Southeast Asian countries. This trend was accelerated after the treaties of the 1840s. Increased foreign commercial contact also brought with it the so-called "coolie trade," a form of contract labour. Western shipping companies engaged in the lucrative business of supplying Chinese labourers to open the California mining areas, to build the Canadian Pacific Railway, and to perform the menial tasks, as well as the hard physical labour, on other similar projects along the North American west coast and in South America.

Those Chinese who remained at home in the southern provinces suffered most from the ravages of opium addiction and from the disruption caused by the new treaty ports. Before 1842, Canton was the only shipping area for foreign buyers of Chinese tea and silks, which came mainly from the south-central Yangtze region. With the opening of new ports farther north—particularly Shanghai—trade routes changed, and the old land-based transport network funnelling these goods down to Canton disappeared, throwing many porters and small merchants into desperate straits. These same provinces had been the last part of the country subdued by the Manchus in the seventeenth century, and they harboured latent anti-Manchu sentiments as well as a newly aroused resentment of foreigners. As local officials in the 1840s proved less and less able to suppress bandits and settle disputes, self-protection associations were organized by either gentry-landlords or secret societies. From one such secret society came the original nucleus of the Taiping's military forces.

The Taiping movement began as a religious society among a minority group, the Hakka, who formed themselves into a military type of structure in self-protection against both official and non-official oppression. What allowed it to spread beyond that minority group and its original locale to become a massive rebellion was a unique quality that also set it apart from earlier Chinese rebellions: namely, a revolutionary ideology that appealed to all discontented peasants and also challenged the traditional Confucian social order. Hung Hsiu-ch'üan, originator and chief philosopher of the movement, was given to religious visions and delusions of grandeur. He had enough classical education to try the official civil-service examinations, but apparently not enough for success, despite three attempts. Influenced by some missionary tracts written in Chinese, and suffering from delirium during an illness following an examination failure, he experienced a series of visions in which he was called upon by God to lead a sacred crusade against the Manchus.

Hung's creed was a mixture of traditional Confucianism's concerns for the peasantry and garbled versions of the Bible. Included was a strong racial nationalism, primarily aimed at the Manchu overlords. He also envisaged a new social order based on co-operative communities. In these, all men and women would share both the land and the fruits of production; the evils of foot-binding, gambling, and opium-smoking would be forbidden. Ultimately, he hoped to set up an earthly paradise. In the meantime, he promised a place in Heaven to all those who fell in the struggle for the ideal society. In support of his religious claims, Hung declared that it had been divinely revealed to him that he was the younger brother of Jesus Christ.

This rebellion posed a direct threat to the traditional position of the Chinese landowning gentry class. The Taiping's economic program struck at the heart of the private landlord who depended on rents for his main income. The rebels' opposition to Confucian classical learning and traditional religious practices further alienated the gentry élite. Besides destroying Taoist and Buddhist temples and images, the Taiping attacked traditional social values by upsetting ancestral tablets in Confucian and clan temples, and even in private homes. In the areas they ruled, their ideology, which some observers called "Taiping Christianity" (though many contemporary missionaries rejected their religious views as non-Christian), replaced the Confucian classics as the curriculum for education and qualification for official office. Whatever their individual feelings concerning the Manchu foreign rulers, the landowners, scholars, and anyone else with a stake in the old system mobilized themselves against this attack on their privileged places in society.

The Taiping Rebellion was a massive upheaval. Within two years of its outbreak in 1851, Taiping forces controlled the strategic Yangtze area, with Nanking as capital of its Heavenly Kingdom of Great Peace. Within the next decade, only two provinces remained untouched by its forces. But the momentum of the movement could not be sustained, because of both external pressure and internal weakness, and after 1856 it was on the wane. A Taiping expeditionary force failed to capture Peking in 1853, permitting the Manchu dynasty to survive and recuperate. Though willing to conduct international trade, the Taiping made foreigners uneasy by denouncing the inequalities of the treaty system. After initial enthusiasm, western missionaries rejected the "heresies" of Taiping Christianity. Inside the movement, growing corruption and nepotism among the leadership sapped the zeal of its peasant supporters.

By the early 1860s the rebels were being steadily pushed back by new, gentry-organized troops, at least partially armed with foreign weaponry and taught by western instructors. In July 1864, Nanking fell. Hung Hsiu-ch'üan was dead, the remaining leaders were executed, and the peasant followers of the Heavenly Kingdom dispersed. It was estimated that 20 million people had died in the long struggle between Taiping armies and imperial forces. The government's treasury was drained and its prestige shaken.

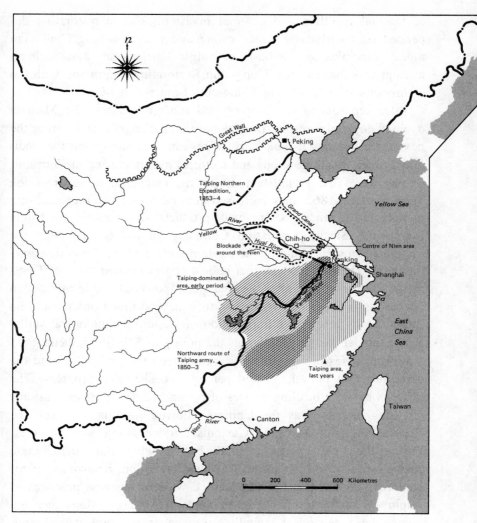

Map 7   The Taiping and Nien Rebellions

The T'ung-chih Restoration and Self-Strengthening

According to the traditional Chinese view of history, a "restoration" of the reigning dynasty might occur if it survived the initial challenge of internal rebellion and external invasion. Such a restoration depended on the dynasty's reaffirming and re-establishing Confucian moral principles as the basis of political behaviour. Just such an attempt was made in the T'ung-chih Restoration, beginning with the enthronement of the young T'ung-chih Emperor in 1861.

After suppressing the Taiping and other rebellions, the Manchu dynasty enjoyed a respite from domestic challengers, and during the next three decades it took steps to revamp and strengthen the traditional order. Machine shops and factories manufacturing modern munitions were first established during the campaign to suppress the Taiping. After 1862, they increased in number and also branched into manufacturing other machine-made products. In the 1870s, the China Merchants' Steam Navigation Company started to challenge the foreign steamships' hold on the modern portion of the domestic carrying trade. The first modern coal-mine complex opened north of Tientsin in 1876, one year after the first steam-powered textile mill began operations in Shanghai. It seemed that the traditional order could be shored up by a selective importation of western technological skills. This approach became known as the policy of Self-Strengthening.

Indeed, assessing the thirty years between the mid-1860s and the mid-1890s, an optimist would perceive considerable progress. The treaty ports were bustling centres of commerce. Government customs revenues increased as the Chinese allowed foreigners to run the Chinese Imperial Maritime Customs Service along western lines. Within the treaty ports, a small but growing class of Chinese businessmen versed in western ways was emerging. Known as "compradores," these men initially learned western business practices as employees of foreign banks and commercial houses. Many then became either independent capitalists or managers for semi-official modern projects such as the China Merchants' Steam Navigation Company. In these years, foreigners acted as instructors, technicians, and translators in several of the modern munitions works. They also staffed the foreign language school, created in the capital in 1862. Missionaries multiplied both within the treaty ports and in the surrounding countryside. Chinese ambassadors were stationed in several western capitals, including London, Washington, and St. Petersburg. Modern studies were officially encouraged as the first students were sent abroad for education, and a growing number of translated western books became available in Chinese. Hope seemed bright that China might ultimately hold her own against the western nations.

A pessimist or cynic, however, would point to the more negative aspects of the economy. He would argue that foreign economic involvement and economic improvement centred almost wholly in a few coastal cities and did not really touch the greatest part of the country. Most foreign capital was invested in commerce and not in establishing native industries. Profits made by foreigners were exported for investment elsewhere. The economic activities of the native compradores followed a very similar pattern. They remained cautious and parasitic, declining involvement in entrepreneurial investment and development. No national economic plan existed. All the modern projects mentioned above were provincially sponsored, and they became semiprivate sources of profit and privilege for the provincial officials who established them. Ventures like the Steam Navigation Company became havens for nepotism and corruption. Native private capital, reluctant to risk money in uncertain undertakings, never relinquished its preference for investment in land or loans. Native investors (whether private or provincial officials) tended to demand quick profits from any new enterprise, and to use these profits for consumer purchasing rather than for reinvestment.

This same pessimistic view would dismiss the Restoration's changes in government attitudes as equally superficial. Foreign diplomacy was still considered a nasty necessity by the court, something inflicted upon the country by foreign military might, and almost uniformly humiliating and disastrous for China's interests. Moreover, a close examination of such institutions as the Tsungli-yamen (created in 1861 to handle all matters relating to foreigners in the capital) would reveal little more than a token adjustment in the old procedures. It could be pointed out that, economically and politically, the foreign presence neither fundamentally affected traditional patterns nor altered traditional practices for the vast majority of the population.

But whether one adopts an optimistic or pessimistic viewpoint, it is clear that a number of significant changes did take place during these years. These stemmed from the Taiping Rebellion. The collapse of the imperial military forces before the first rebel attacks left the dynasty dependent on new provincial armies hurriedly raised by local Confucian scholar-officials and gentry. Some of the officials who raised these forces became governors-general or governors, the highest positions within the provincial bureaucracy. It was they who purchased or built the first modern arsenals, guns, and steamships. In turn, the new armies and their officers gave their political loyalty directly to these high provincial officials who supplied their needs from the provincial treasury. Governors-general and governors often took over the task of choosing army officers and lower officials, and they cared less about the ability of these men to pass the official examinations than about their personal reliability and skill in combining military leadership and civilian administrative expertise. These new officers and officials were all native Chinese, upsetting the Manchu rulers' careful balance between Manchus and Chinese in high provincial posts. Military and civil authority was combined in such officials, and a great deal of power now lay within provincial rather than central court circles.

The Manchu court reluctantly adjusted to the new armies with their attached provincial circle of minor officials and independent economic support systems. One such army was moved north in 1866 to suppress the Nien rebels, and another was sent to suppress the Moslem uprisings in the northwest and the Moslem independence movement in Chinese Turkestan. The Nien (meaning ''bands'') had never developed the type of internal organizational strength that marked the Taiping movement. Centred in the region just south of the Yellow River, they remained a looser confederation of allied rebel groups. Traditional Chinese peasant grievances and secret-society oaths and rituals (particularly those of the White Lotus Society) formed their only bond. The Nien rebellions, like the religious Moslem uprisings, provided further indications of the extent of popular discontent and the growing weakness of the Manchu central government. The Ch'ing armies collapsed at the rebels' initial challenge. The rebels, however, were unable to reconcile their differences with each other into a single anti-Manchu effort, and their separate rebellions allowed the Confucian scholar-gentry time to organize their own provincial forces. By the end of the 1870s, China had been "pacified." The new-style armies had proven themselves effective; in fact, they were the only really effective forces within the empire.

The abilities of these new Chinese provincial officials were personified in Li Hung-chang. He had raised a highly effective army in his native province of Anhwei during the Taiping suppression campaigns, and later this army (under one of Li's protégés) also crushed the Nien rebels. Li became governor-general at Tientsin in 1870 and held that post until 1895. This long tenure in a single office was a marked departure from the traditional practice of frequent rotation to prevent any one official from building up a semi-independent power base —such as Li, in fact, created. During his long official residence in Tientsin, Li followed a policy of Self-Strengthening and established a bureaucratic network of capable personal followers. The first native steamship company, the first modern coal mine, the first telegraph system, and the first steam textile mill were launched through his initiative and support. During most of this period he was also, unofficially, the nearest approximation of a foreign minister within the empire, a role more indicative of court confidence and foreign trust than any official position he held. The career of Li and others like him marked a fundamental shift in the traditional political balance of power between Manchu and Chinese, and between the central government and the provinces.

To understand why this realignment of power did not eventually eclipse the Manchu overlordship, it is necessary to look at the incredible figure known as Empress Dowager Tz'u-hsi. In 1851, at seventeen years of age, she became a low-ranking concubine of the Hsien-feng Emperor. She accompanied the Emperor nine years later in flight from Peking when Anglo-French forces invaded north China to secure their demands for altered treaty relations. Before the refugee court returned to the capital in 1861, the Hsien-feng Emperor was dead, leaving the throne to his only son, then five years old. The new T'ung-chih

Emperor was the offspring of his father's young concubine, who was now raised to the status of Empress Dowager and given the formal name of Tz'u-hsi, by which she is best known. By 1865 this ultra-conservative, stubborn, uneducated, but incredibly ambitious and determined woman was the most powerful figure in the empire. So she remained, by fair means and foul, until her death in 1908. In 1875, upon the mysterious death of her son soon after he reached the age of majority, Tz'u-hsi defied the succession laws of the Manchu royal line and enthroned a four-year-old nephew. Her carefully constructed net-

Li Hung-chang (1823–1901) with British Prime Minister and Foreign Secretary Lord Salisbury (left) and Lord Curzon, Under-Secretary for Foreign Affairs, during world tour in 1896.

The Empress Dowager Tz'u-hsi, who from 1860 until her death in 1908 dominated Manchu court politics.

work of allies in the palace, in government offices, and among the capital troops, made certain her choice was upheld. With a minor on the throne, Tz'u-hsi was once again Regent, until 1889.

Dedicated to the survival of the Manchus, Tz'u-hsi nevertheless accepted the growth of the regional power bases. While she recognized their potential threat, she also appreciated their usefulness in the absence of any central government troops of sufficient military capacity to maintain order. She depended on the loyalty of Li Hung-chang and other governors-general, trusting that they would be bound by tradition to the ruling dynasty. She turned out to be correct, for these proponents of the Self-Strengthening policy remained motivated by the conservative Confucianism of the "restoration" concept. Those same Confucian loyalties prevented them from developing their regional power bases into truly independent or challenging political units. Thus the court was able to retain a central role and to play off one regional leader against the other, a game at which Tz'u-hsi proved a consummate master. Thus these semi-independent provincial complexes did not bring about the downfall of the traditional imperial system. They did, however, profoundly influence China's search for an alternative system in the early twentieth century.

Analysis

1. Discuss the validity of either one of the following hypotheses: (a) The Taiping Rebellion failed because it did not contain the necessary ingredients to turn a rebellion into a revolution; (b) The Taiping Rebellion was doomed to failure because its ideals conflicted too deeply with Chinese traditions.

2. Assess the Self-Strengthening movement of the Manchus as an adequate response to peasant discontent and foreign intervention.

3. In what ways did China's economic development in the last half of the nineteenth century follow a traditional type of "colonial pattern"?

4. To what extent has your country's economic development in the nineteenth and twentieth centuries followed similar lines?

5. What economic alternatives existed for China in this period? Explain why none of these alternatives developed.

6. Why did the author entitle this chapter "Century of Shame: The Inner Realm"? Do you agree that this is an appropriate choice? Why?

Suggested Readings

J. O. P. Bland and E. Backhouse, *China Under the Empress Dowager* (Philadelphia: Lippincott, 1910; reprint, Taipei: Literature House, 1962). (Hardcover)

   A standard reference on the period of Tz'u-hsi's domination of Chinese political life, its value is great, although its choice of Chinese materials for translated portions is often questionable and undocumented.

J. M. Gibson and D. M. Johnston, eds., *A Century of Struggle: Canadian Essays on Revolutionary China* (Toronto: Canadian Institute of International Relations, 1971).

   Two chapters in particular: J. J. Gerson, "Rebellions in Pre-revolutionary Times," and B. L. Evans, "Reformism versus Conservatism, 1840–1911," provide useful short essays for discussion.

Hsüeh Chün-tu, ed., *Revolutionary Leaders of Modern China* (London: Oxford University Press, 1971).

   Four chapters in Section 1, "The Taiping Rebellion," contain excellent short studies of this movement's leaders.

Jason Wong, ed., *China in the 19th Century: Selected Sources* (Toronto: McClelland & Stewart Ltd., 1971).

   A good, short selection of translated documents covering mainly the Opium War, Taiping Rebellion, and Self-Strengthening era, and the Reform Movement and Boxer Rebellion in the 1890s.

SECTION II   SUMMARY AND RESEARCH

1. Historians usually discover a number of causes for historical events. Many historians then rank and interpret these causes. What causes does the author present for western imperialism in this period? How does he rank or interpret them? Do you agree? Was the underlying factor of social and political unrest in China from 1840 to 1911 a growing nationalism based on the hatred of foreigners?

2. Account for the general inability of the Chinese to react effectively to the growing internal and external pressures.

3. Rewrite from a Chinese point of view the section in Chapter 7 which deals with the Opium War. If you were teaching this section to a class in modern China today, what ideas would you emphasize?

4. Compare the Taiping Rebellion to any other pre-modern rebellion you have studied. What do these revolts have in common? Explain the differences.

5. Explain why Japan's response to western imperialism was different from China's.

SECTION III
THE SEARCH FOR
RESPECTABILITY

CHAPTER 9
Reform, Rebellion, or Revolution?

Chronology

1876 Japan opens Korea for foreign trade and residence.

1885 Li-Itō agreement reducing threat of Sino-Japanese conflict over Korea.

1894–5 Sino-Japanese War sparked by Korean Rebellion.

1896 Russia gains right to build Chinese Eastern Railway across Manchuria as shortcut link in Trans-Siberian Railway begun in 1891.

1897 Russian seizure and lease of Port Arthur; German lease of Tsingtao in Shantung; British lease of New Territories and Weihaiwei; French lease of Kwangchow Bay.

1898 Hundred Days of Reform.

1899–1900 Boxer Rebellion, Allied Expedition, and Russian advances in Manchuria.

1904–5 Russo-Japanese War.

1905–6 Abolition of traditional examination system.

1908 Announcement of drafting of Constitution; death of Empress Dowager Tz'u-hsi; enthronement of three-year-old Emperor (Henry) P'u-i under regency of father.

1910 Korea absorbed into Japanese Empire.

The uneasy relationship between traditional cultural forces and modern influences from the West became a confrontation in the fateful decades between 1890 and 1925. The range of opinion in this confused period is indicated by the following:[25]

The views of Chang Chih-tung (1837–1909), a prominent Self-Strengthening provincial official and chief rival of Li Hung-chang:

Scholars today must master the classics first, in order to understand the purpose underlying the establishment of education by our ancient Chinese sages and teachers. They must study history, in order to learn the rise and fall of succeeding dynasties of China, and the customs of the empire. They must glance over the philosophical works and belles-lettres in order to become thoroughly familiar with Chinese academic ideas and exquisite writings. And then they can select and make use of that Western knowledge which can make up our shortcomings, and adopt those Western methods of government which can cure our illnesses. (1898)

The views of T'an Ssu-t'ung (1865–98), a young radical thinker who became a martyr of the Hundred Days of Reform:

Your idea of despising our enemies arises because you think that they are still barbarians. . . . We must first make ourselves respectable before we despise others. Now there is not a single one of the Chinese people's sentiments, customs, or political and legal institutions which can be favourably compared with those of the barbarians. (1898?)

A public notice of the Boxer Rebellion:

Attention: All people in markets and villages of all provinces in China —now, owing to the fact that Catholics and Protestants have vilified our gods and sages, have deceived our emperors and ministers above, and oppressed the Chinese people below, both our gods and our people are angry at them, yet we have to keep silent. This forces us to practise the I-ho magic boxing so as to protect our country, expel the foreign bandits and kill Christian converts, in order to save our people from miserable suffering. (1899)

The views of Hu Han-min (1879–1936), a revolutionary and a prominent leader in Sun Yat-sen's Kuomintang, or Nationalist Party:

For the sake of our independence and salvation, we must overthrow the Manchu dynasty. The Manchus have hurt the Chinese people so much that there has arisen an inseparable barrier between them. . . . Those who advocate assimilation of the Manchus without having them overthrown merely serve as tools of the tyrannical dynasty and are therefore shameless to the utmost. . . . But unless their political power is overthrown, the Chinese nation will forever remain the conquered people without independence, and, being controlled by a backward nation, will finally perish with it in the struggle with the advanced foreign powers. (1906)

The accommodation of past tradition with modern technology, the acceptance of foreign superiority in defiance of traditional views, the violent rejection of foreign influence, or revolution in the name of Chinese nationalism—these were the main currents of debate within the crucial years when the shape of twentieth-century China began to emerge.

Korea and the Clash with Asian Modernity

Korea had for centuries been an important cultural bridge between Japan and China, and in the mid-nineteenth century it was the highest-ranked tributary state in the traditional Chinese hierarchic world order. (Tributary states were those countries which, in Chinese eyes, possessed sufficient cultural advancement to acknowledge Chinese superiority by periodic ceremonial presentations of tribute or native products to the Chinese emporer. In return, the visiting tribute mission received the emperor's expression of kindly concern, his formal acknowledgment of the legitimacy of their rulers' authority, return gifts, and the right to conduct private trade.) Challenged in the 1860s by a peasant rebellion strikingly similar to the Taiping movement, native Korean leaders responded with a persecution of Christianity and a reassertion of traditional Confucian values borrowed centuries before from China. In keeping with custom and its tributary status, Korea left all foreign relations to Peking, and all western efforts to penetrate this ''hermit kingdom'' were rejected by force.

Korea's close neighbour, Japan, had for two centuries also refused outside trade and contact (except for limited rights granted to Dutch and Chinese traders), but western pressure had forced it to abandon seclusion after 1854. In 1868, Japan abandoned its traditional feudal order and embarked on a course of rapid modernization under the rule of the Meiji Emperor (1868–1911). Subjected in the 1850s to unequal treaties, similar to those imposed on China by western powers, Japan was determined to rid itself of these by equalling and surpassing western countries in wealth and power. Japan also sought to emulate the imperialist spirit of the western powers. In 1876, a Japanese fleet forced entry into the hermit kingdom and imposed unequal treaty arrangements on Korea. Thus Korea was drawn into its unenviable modern position at the centre of contending imperialistic ambitions in northeast Asia.

From the 1880s on, Korean politics were a confusing mixture of quarrelling internal factions and foreign interference. Die-hard native conservatives fought with radical groups, while Japanese and Chinese agents manoeuvred against each other in competition for court advisory roles to strengthen their influence over Korean politics. American diplomats and missionaries joined with those of other western nations to stimulate and aid native Korean elements seeking modernity and independence. In 1885, Li Hung-chang met with Prime Minister Itō of Japan and worked out an agreement to reduce the mounting threat of Sino-Japanese confrontation within Korea. In 1894, however, when a domestic rebellion of conservative reformists broke out in Korea, that agreement broke down. Both Chinese and Japanese intervention in the Korean rebellion led to direct armed conflict between the two major powers.

The battles of the Sino-Japanese War of 1894–5 were essentially a test of Japanese against Chinese modernization, and the quick resolution of that contest surprised foreign powers as much as China. Japanese forces speedily seized the initiative in Korea and then spilled over into Manchuria. In a rapid series of naval encounters in the fall of 1894, the Japanese navy virtually destroyed Li Hung-chang's modern naval forces. The peace settlement of 1895 and the commercial agreement of 1896 were a humiliating climax to the unequal treaty system for China. Besides paying a large indemnity and ceding Taiwan and the Pescadores Islands to the Japanese Empire, China was forced to grant Japan all treaty rights previously accorded to western powers. Some refinements were added as well, such as the opening of more treaty ports and the granting of rights to establish tax-free industries within the treaty ports. Finally, Korea was declared independent of China's traditional suzerainty. A further decade of competing foreign influences in Korea, this time between Japanese and Russian agents, led to war between these two countries in 1904. As a result of the Japanese victory in 1905, Korea formally became a protectorate of Japan. Five years later, continued Korean efforts to regain independence brought down upon it the wrath of Japan and ended in the official incorporation of Korea within the Japanese Empire.

Western powers, taking advantage of China's demonstrated weakness, lost no time in pressing for more privileges. In what was called the "scramble for concessions," they demanded that the Chinese lease to them certain territories, and around these they created "spheres of influence." Russia secured such a sphere of influence in southern Manchuria, centring on her lease of Port Arthur; Germany moved into Tsingtao on the Shantung peninsula; and France created her area of influence at Kwangchow Bay in south China (see Map 8). Characteristically, the dominant commercial nation in China's foreign trade, Britain, outdid them all by leasing the New Territories opposite Hong Kong for ninety-nine years, securing a naval base at Weihaiwei in Shantung, and claiming the entire Yangtze region as its sphere of influence. Legitimized by new treaties, these leased territories differed from the treaty port concessions in several ways. Each belonged to a single country. The surrounding spheres of influence were consolidated not by direct foreign control but rather by a whole series of new bilateral arrangements which granted the western countries special privileges in their spheres, such as railway construction rights, mining concessions, manufacturing permits, and guarantees of participation in the lucrative field of foreign loans to the Chinese government. The threat of outright partition and the fear of sinking into colonial status began to loom large in the minds of many Chinese.

Within China, the 1895 defeat by tiny Japan, a former Asian tributary country, and the resulting new phase of privileges to western imperialists were fatal shocks to the comfortable feeling that Self-Strengthening was sufficient protection against further foreign intrusions. Numerous study and discussion societies sprang up, and they conducted heated debates everywhere through a new wave of popular journals and newspapers. Sympathetic provincial officials, and the immunity of the foreign concessions from the Chinese authorities, protected these societies and their publications from sporadic attempts by the central government to enforce the traditional ban on policy discussions outside formal bureaucratic circles. The fate of China was

Map 8   The Manchu Dynasty

now a matter of broad public concern and debate, rather than the sole business of Peking officialdom.

The debate took on greater momentum as more and more was learned about western nations. The first serious efforts toward educating Chinese students abroad were undertaken in these years, and the first effects of foreign education were soon felt within Chinese intellectual circles. Yen Fu (1853–1921) provides the most prominent example. After preliminary training in the traditional Confucian curriculum, he was selected to study English language and naval subjects at the Foochow shipyard, an institution typical of those that had been set up to effect the Self-Strengthening policy initiated in the Taiping period. He graduated in 1871, and between 1877 and 1879 he studied at the Greenwich Naval College in England. On his return he was attached to Li Hung-chang's new Peiyang Naval Academy at Tientsin, although his own views never coincided with Li's more cautious accommodation to western ideas. The Sino-Japanese War released Yen Fu's pent-up frustrations, and the stream of writings that flowed from him after 1895 reflected the new sense of urgency felt by Chinese intellectuals. Yen Fu began, through newspaper and book translations, to introduce Chinese readers to the ideas of western thinkers such as Adam Smith, T. H. Huxley, John Stuart Mill, and Herbert Spencer. Through Yen Fu and others, western concepts in politics, society, and economics (as well as the superiority of western technology) became part of an on-going discussion in China.

The first major political thrust of this new intellectual wave came in 1895 when K'ang Yu-wei (1858–1927) and his equally brilliant student, Liang Ch'i-ch'ao (1873–1929), mobilized the twelve hundred candidates who were in the capital for the civil-service examinations and presented to the throne a joint memorial (the traditional form of written communication to the emperor). The memorial advocated both rejection of the Japanese peace-treaty terms and the moving of the capital inland to continue the struggle. It went on to suggest a host of reforms, ranging from an end to the lucrative sale of official degrees to the opening of agricultural and business schools. The suggestions were of course rejected, but the memorial indicated the sweeping scope of possible changes in the traditional order that already existed in the minds of many Chinese.

K'ang Yu-wei shocked conservative Confucian scholars by his erudite, devastating attacks on the authenticity of several revered Confucian classics. Although this prevented him from securing an official bureaucratic posting, his enemies could not prevent recognition of his superb intellect. He was appointed a Hanlin academician, an honorary designation reserved for the most renowned scholars of the empire. Following this honour, K'ang began to rethink time-honoured Chinese traditions. He rejected the common view of Confucius as a conservative who advocated following the examples of ancient sage-kings. K'ang instead depicted him as a liberal reformer who had fabricated the myths of the past Golden Age in order to persuade his contemporaries to undertake reforms. In K'ang's hands, China's classical learning was reinterpreted or twisted to support the concepts of change and progress.

In 1898, K'ang Yu-wei and his compatriots had a brief moment of political opportunity in what came to be called the Hundred Days of Reform. The youthful Emperor (now twenty-four years old) had been freed from the stern, directing hand of his aging aunt, the Empress Dowager, upon her retirement in 1889. Still caught within the very limiting environment of the court, the Emperor increasingly indicated serious interest in government matters. In 1898, through the Emperor's tutor, K'ang and his group gained access to the Emperor and persuaded him to create a new China by imperial fiat. With stunning rapidity, between June 11 and September 21, 1898, an avalanche of edicts declared war on the traditional establishment, both at the centre and in the provinces. In sweeping proclamations, the Emperor promised a constitutional monarchy with representative institutions, a modern bureaucracy, and a new, progressive economic system. These measures not only frightened conservatives but alienated even moderate reformers.

Most officials simply bided their time, awaiting the reaction of the Empress Dowager. Having retired officially in 1889, she nevertheless maintained intact her political network, which included court eunuchs, Manchu princes, and conservative Chinese officials. As the upholders of Manchu privilege, classical learning, and organized corruption, these groups were the direct targets of the reformers. Thus, most officials and scholars were relieved when the Empress Dowager, on September 21, imprisoned the Emperor within the palace and re-

established her regency. Six of the reformers were executed. K'ang
Yu-wei and Liang Ch'i-ch'ao fled to Japan. From exile, Liang, in
particular, poured out a constant stream of writings about the West
which influenced thousands of young Chinese.

The last years of Tz'u-hsi's power witnessed a rising confrontation
between the forces of tradition and the forces of change, with the
Manchu establishment trying to maintain its position under increasingly difficult circumstances. In some circles, anti-foreign, and especially anti-Christian, sentiments reached new heights. Fanned among
the populace by conservative local gentry, these feelings were directed
particularly at the new influx of western missionaries in the interior of
the country. The missionaries, on their part, could not easily ap-
preciate the Chinese attitude. As one leading Protestant noted in
commenting about the local gentry:

*A Canadian missionary in the China Inland Mission compound c. 1906 in Shanghai.
The ricksha-puller is an uncharacteristically well-groomed "coolie".*

It is impossible not to displease them. To preach is to insult them, for in the very act you assume the position of a teacher. To publish a book on religion or science is to insult them, for in doing that you take for granted that China is not the depository of all truth and knowledge. . . . To propound progress is to insult them, for therein you intimate that China has not reached the very acme of civilization, and that you stand on a higher platform than they.[26]

Suspicion and resentment were heightened by Chinese converts to Christianity, who often acted independently of traditional local social solidarity. The defeat by the Japanese, the scramble for concessions by foreign powers, and the depressed economic conditions in the countryside all added to the resentment of foreigners and of the dynasty.

This anti-foreign and anti-Christian sentiment exploded in the Boxer Rebellion. In 1898, in parts of Chihli and Shantung provinces particularly hard hit by floods and famine, an old secret society, known as the *I-ho ch'üan* (to westerners simply the Boxers), spearheaded a full-scale peasant uprising. Originally, their political program included the overthrow of the Manchu dynasty, as well as the expulsion of foreigners and the killing of all Christian converts. However, after initial skirmishes with imperial troops, an informal alliance was formed between the Boxers and arch-conservative officials of the Empress Dowager's own court circle. The rebels pillaged and plundered Christian missions, murdered converts, and proclaimed that they were supporting the dynasty by ridding the country of all foreign influences. The Empress Dowager apparently secretly hoped that the Boxers might succeed. In June 1900, as Boxer mobs surrounded the foreign legation quarters in Peking and Tientsin, the court issued a pronouncement that amounted to a declaration of war on all foreign powers in China.

Luckily for the dynasty, Li Hung-chang and other high provincial leaders ignored the order and persuaded the foreigners to regard all but the northern provinces as neutral territory. The foreign powers put together a combined military force, which came to the relief of the foreign concessions in Tientsin in mid-July and the Peking legation quarter in mid-August. As in 1860, the imperial court fled the city, which was looted by the triumphant foreign troops. Li Hung-chang negotiated the humiliating surrender terms on behalf of the absent Manchu court.

A Sino-foreign protocol issued on September 7, 1901, accepted the fiction of the uprising as a rebellion rather than a court-sanctioned war. Thus Tz'u-hsi and the court were able to return to the capital and officially thank the foreign powers for their assistance in restoring order. Nevertheless, the foreigners levied a staggering indemnity, amounting in total to some 330 million dollars. While no more than one-third of the sum was ever paid, it was worth noting that interest rates on the foreign loans required by China would have doubled the original figure before the final payment deadline of 1940.

Conservative reformism had a last, brief fling following the Boxer catastrophe. The indomitable Tz'u-hsi mounted a reform program that sought to retain Manchu predominance within a gradually reconstructed political format. Although the actual political reforms were only slowly implemented, one fundamental change did occur: the old-style civil-service examinations (the bulwark of the Confucian bureaucratic order) gave way to a modern system of formal schooling through primary, secondary, and university levels. The Empress Dowager, or "Old Buddha" as she was popularly known, died in 1908, mysteriously preceded twenty-four hours earlier by her nephew, the Emperor whom she had raised to the throne and dominated thereafter. Another infant, (Henry) P'u-i, was placed on the Dragon Throne, this time under the regency of the most conservative Manchu princes, headed by his father. In April 1911, the princes announced a new cabinet system of government on the western model, but the cabinet members included only four Chinese, with eight Manchus (five were imperial relatives) and one Mongol (Mongols had formed a close alliance with the Manchus before the latter's conquest of China in 1644, and thereafter had constantly held high posts in the Ch'ing central bureaucracy). The old system proved incapable of substantial internal adjustment, and reform soon gave way to revolution in twentieth-century China.

Analysis

1. Explain why the four different views (stated on pages 104–5) could emerge at approximately the same time to deal with the problem of China's salvation. Consider the validity of each view. Select the point of view which you consider to be the most reasonable. Prepare a defence of your selection.

2. In a time of crisis the usual reactions are to modernize or to return to established traditions. Debate the two options for China around 1900. What groups would support each side? Why?

3. The author entitled the chapter "Reform, Rebellion, or Revolution?". Prepare an argument for each of these alternatives for the years 1890 to 1911.

4. Account for the failure of reform and rebellion.

Suggested Readings

James B. Crowley, ed., *Modern East Asia: Essays in Interpretation* (New York: Harcourt, Brace & World, 1970).
   This collection of essays on various periods of modern East Asian history contains a valuable chapter on this period by Ernest P. Young, entitled "Nationalism, Reform, and Republican Revolution: China in the Early Twentieth Century."

Hsüeh Chün-tu, ed., *Revolutionary Leaders of Modern China* (London: Oxford University Press, 1971).
   Chapters 5–8 give a good panoramic coverage of this period and of the early revolutionary figures.

Jessie G. Lutz, ed., *Christian Missions: Evangelists of What?* (Boston: Heath, 1965).
   A useful collection of various Chinese and western views on the controversial role of western missionaries in the modern history of China.

Chester C. Tan, *The Boxer Catastrophe* (New York Columbia University Press, 1955). (Hardcover)
   A good study with emphasis on diplomatic relations during this critical period.

CHAPTER 10
Revolution in Crisis

Chronology

1911 "Double Ten" uprising at Wuchang (October 10).

1912 Sun Yat-sen inaugurated as Provisional President of Republic of China (January 1); abdication of last emperor (February 12); Yuan Shih-k'ai inaugurated as President (March 10).

1913 "Second Revolution" by Sun Yat-sen's forces fails.

1915–16 Yuan Shih-k'ai declares himself Emperor and rescinds restoration of monarchy after storm of protest; the death of Yuan.

1917 Bolshevik Revolution in Russia.

1919 Student protest against Versailles Peace Conference (May 4).

1921 Sun Yat-sen establishes rival government at Canton, challenging warlord-dominated Peking government (April 2); Chinese Communist Party founded.

1924 First National Congress of reorganized Kuomintang (Nationalist Party) at Canton (January 20–30).

1925 Sun Yat-sen dies in Peking (March 12).

In the early twentieth century, a rising spirit of Chinese nationalism formed the core of revolutionary sentiment. From the start, this nationalism had a strong flavour of anti-imperialism. At the same time, the attraction of Britain and other European countries as models for modernization declined as two new world powers—the United States and Soviet Russia—without the apparent taint of imperialism, began to influence Chinese thinking.

Initially, the United States was the more attractive to many Chinese. Dynamic, successful, and idealistic, the United States had played only a minor role in the western battering of Chinese seclusion in the early nineteenth century. In the 1890s, rather than scrambling for concessions, America had denounced the Old World nations and espoused an "open-door policy" which insisted on equal foreign access to trade and investment, even within the spheres of influence. Later, radical Chinese nationalism would condemn this policy as merely a cover for the aggressive competitiveness of American capital export. But it was not so regarded in this period.

Soviet Russia's influence in China followed the success of the Bolshevik Revolution. The overthrow of the Tsarist regime in 1917 had a profound effect upon all areas of the world, particularly those under western imperialist domination. The Soviet model, promising rapid domestic rejuvenation and freedom from foreign control, immediately attracted attention in China. The course of Chinese history in the twentieth century reflects the continuous dual influences of the United States and Russia.

The Partial Revolution

The first prominent figure on whom those influences operated was Sun Yat-sen (1866–1925), revered by Chinese of every political persuasion as the Father of Modern China. The son of a peasant farmer near Macao, his early education came from an uncle who had fought in the Taiping Rebellion. As a young teenager, Sun lived with an older brother in Honolulu, where he attended an Anglican school and became a Christian. Further study in Hong Kong gained him a medical degree from a British mission hospital. However, in the mid-1890s Sun abandoned medicine to devote himself to the cause of revolution, which, he believed, was the only path to China's salvation.

Sun's early revolutionary efforts proved fruitless. He organized his first secret underground group in 1894, and tried the following year to seize government offices in Canton. The venture failed and Sun went into exile in Europe and America. These years in western countries helped to clarify his ideas on revolutionary theory. He also began to win international renown as a symbol of anti-Manchu sentiment. In 1897 he was kidnapped by Chinese embassy staff members in London, but British public opinion, mobilized by an old English teacher he had known in Hong Kong, forced his release. Travelling widely in the western world and Japan, Sun spent most of the first decade of this century soliciting funds from Chinese who were permanently resident abroad, or "overseas Chinese," negotiating with rival revolutionary societies, and synthesizing an ideology suitable for a Chinese Republic. The result of this thinking and experience was his Three Principles of the People, or *San Min Chu I*—Nationalism, Democracy, and People's Livelihood. The first principle contained the strongest rallying cry, expressed in the manifesto of his new revolutionary brotherhood in 1905 as "China is the China of the Chinese."[27] However, Sun's revolutionary group continued to meet with failure in frequent efforts to organize a successful uprising in China.

Despite numerous societies like Sun's, the actual revolution, when it came in 1911, surprised revolutionaries as well as Manchus. A minor military revolt on October 10 (the "Double Ten" Uprising), 1911, in Wuchang, an industrial city in the mid-Yangtze, prompted several provinces quickly to declare their independence from the Manchu central government in Peking. Within three months, various coalitions of army officers, provincial assembly members, and leaders of revolutionary associations controlled all the southern, central, and northwestern provinces. Little fighting took place, and little unity existed between the various provinces. The only core was an embryonic Chinese Republic at Nanking, supported in varying degrees by most of the rebellious provinces and a variety of revolutionary secret societies. Sun was in Denver, Colorado, when the Wuchang uprising broke out, and upon reading about it in the newspaper he hurried back to China and was inaugurated as Provisional President of the new Republic of China on January 1, 1912.

The Manchu court placed its fate in the hands of Yuan Shih-k'ai (1859–1916). A former protégé of Li Hung-chang, Yuan had succeeded his mentor as governor-general of Tientsin on Li's death in 1901. There, Yuan had created the strongest modern army in the nation. He had no particular love for the Manchu princes, who had tried to curb his growing power. When Sun Yat-sen offered him the presidency in return for his support of the infant Republic, Yuan

(Henry) P'u-i (1906–67), the last emperor of China, dethroned in 1911; this photograph was taken in 1934 on the eve of his enthronement as emperor of the Japanese puppet state of Manchukuo.

Yuan Shih-k'ai (1859–1916), military strongman and President of the Republic of China, 1912–16. The calligraphy is Yuan's name, written by his own hand.

secured the abdication of the last Manchu emperor and, in early March 1912, became President of the Republic of China. Thus did the Ch'ing dynasty collapse after 267 years, and with it went the Confucian monarchy that for many centuries had been the keystone of China's political structure.

Yuan Shih-k'ai was neither a democrat nor a revolutionary. His refusal of military support to the reformers in 1898 had spelt their final collapse before the Empress Dowager's counter-coup. Nevertheless Sun Yat-sen had hoped that Yuan's authoritarian tendencies would be restrained by the new political parties and the new representative institutions of the Republic embodied in the Provisional Constitution passed in early 1912. The next four years proved how vain were these hopes. Yuan moved the capital from Nanking back to his familiar power base at Peking. He practised corruption on a grand scale, used strong-arm tactics to repress opposition, and revised the Constitution at will. International recognition of his government was utilized mainly to gain loans, which he used to sustain his personal position. In 1913 he easily defeated the Second Revolution, when some provincial governors acted with Sun Yat-sen's revolutionaries to challenge Yuan's increasing autocracy.

Yuan moved quickly through short stages from dictator to President-for-Life. In early 1916, he had his supporters organize a ''popular'' campaign for his enthronement as founder of a new imperial dynasty. Restoration of the monarchy proved one step beyond public tolerance, however, and widespread hostility defeated that effort. Yuan died in mid-1916. Conservative monarchists tried to restore the last Ch'ing emperor in 1917, but this also failed. The Confucian imperial system was defunct, although the revolution had not yet produced a viable alternative.

Following Yuan Shih-k'ai's death, the country rapidly descended into chaos. Yuan had held a semblance of central control. Military governors in all regions were tied to him personally through patronage and the threat of force. With him gone, this fragile unifying strand disappeared. An official government continued in Peking, but it became little more than a focus of international diplomacy and an arena for political intrigues by regional military cliques. Each region fell under the sway of a local military strongman whose power depended on his strength and skill in the confusing politics of alliances and incessant warfare among warlords. With the dominance of the warlords from 1917 to 1927, nationalistic hopes for a new order received a serious setback. These developments convinced Sun Yat-sen that more than a vague nationalism and a faith in republican principles were needed for a successful revolution.

A New Revolutionary Party and a New Revolutionary Culture

Excluded from power by Yuan and his successors, Sun became the guiding spirit of a number of revolutionary groups which combined to form the Kuomintang, or Nationalist Party. The revolutionary forces had hoped that the western powers would assist them in establishing a democratic republic, but the refusal of the western powers to aid them against the warlord-dominated Peking government fanned anti-western sentiment within the new Nationalist Party. Revolutionary Russia was more sympathetic, providing arms and advisers to Sun's organization.

In the early 1920s the Kuomintang (KMT) was reorganized. Its model was the Russian Communist Party, in which tight party discipline was exercised at various levels, from local cells to a central executive committee that had absolute authority. Based in Canton, this new movement shared a shaky control of the region with various local warlords. A Party institute trained political agents in the techniques of organizing mass public support for the coming revolution. A series of lectures by Sun in the winter of 1923–4 set down explicitly his Three Principles of the People as the ideology of the Party. Theoretically, every Party member was indoctrinated with his program. However, later events showed that, in many cases, lip service rather than a real commitment was the result.

Allied to the Party structure, as distinct from the state structure, a Party army was organized which drew its leadership from a new military academy at Whampoa, just outside Canton. Several names of later importance were connected with the Whampoa Academy

Sun Yat-sen (1867–1925), the father of republicanism in China, with his wife Soong Ching-ling, who is a sister of Mme Chiang Kai-shek and at present (1977) one of the vice-chairmen of the People's Republic of China.

—Chiang Kai-shek (the Academy's Commandant), Chou En-lai (Deputy Head of the Political Education Department), and Lin Piao (one of the Academy's early graduates). The last two belong to the history of the Chinese Communist Party. Their presence here reflects the temporary alliance in a "united front," under Russian orders, of the infant Chinese Communist Party (CCP), formed in 1921, and Sun's Kuomintang.

The reorganization of the KMT was completed and the political agents and military forces were ready to launch their Northern Expedition to unify the country when, on March 12, 1925, Sun Yat-sen died. He had gone to Peking in one last fruitless effort to persuade the militarist government to surrender peacefully to the republican forces. With his sudden death, the Kuomintang was deprived of the key element in its internal unity.

Paralleling the growing political revolution in these years was a separate movement which sought to apply revolution to culture. The cry for a cultural revolution came particularly from a group of scholars and students at Peking National University (Peita) between 1917 and 1921. Many of the group had experienced both a Confucian education in China and a western education abroad. They believed that China's hope for progress lay in a new, national culture, free from both restrictive tradition and slavish imitations of foreign cultures.

The ideas expressed by this movement were very diverse, and their effect reached far beyond any narrow circles. "Mr. Science" and "Mr. Democracy" became capsule slogans of the movement, summarizing its challenge to all traditional ways of thought and behaviour. Campaigns were organized to combat footbinding, opium addiction, and the traditional family authoritarianism. Instead of studying in order to achieve family prestige and political position, many students now became social activists who challenged some of the fundamental premises of the old family system. Publications of the movement were written in *pai-hua* Chinese, the "simple" vernacular of the spoken word, and not in the complex *ku-wen*, the classical literary style of the Confucian scholarly tradition. Adult literacy classes were opened throughout the country. Novels and short stories, traditionally downgraded by the élite, became favourite means of spreading ideas of social reform. The new culture was to be a popular one within the grasp of the masses, and not just for a small literate élite. Never tightly organized, the cultural-revolution movement was perhaps more pervasive in its influence than the new political-party movement established by Sun Yat-sen.

Nationalism was the central motivating force of the cultural movement, just as it was within the political movement. The world's ideas were combed for inspiration, and almost every western ideology found advocates in China. But the common motivation was a search for a Chinese solution to China's problems. To borrow without loss of identity, to modernize without westernizing, these were the primary aims of the cultural movement.

This nationalistic bond was demonstrated in the incident in 1919 that gave the cultural revolution its title of the May Fourth Movement. Diplomats of the world's major powers were meeting at Versailles, France, to settle on peace terms after the First World War. Their discussions revealed that secret wartime agreements had been made to win Japanese support for the Allies. The Versailles Conference confirmed these agreements, allowing Japan to retain defeated Germany's unequal treaty rights in China. The conference also made public the Peking warlord government's complicity in these wartime arrangements. Even American President Woodrow Wilson seemingly deserted China's cause, reluctantly abandoning his stirring advocacy of open diplomacy and national self-determination for the sake of a united peace agreement. In the eyes of Chinese nationalists, a European war, supposedly fought for democratic principles, had resulted in a peace agreement that patently denied justice to China, which had hoped to see an end to all unequal treaties. On May 4, 1919, Peking students led by the group at Peking National University responded to these revelations with a mass protest march.

The Peking warlord government ordered the arrest of the student demonstrators, touching off a wave of national sympathy that included student strikes, merchant boycotts, and a massive general strike in Shanghai. The ferment forced the government to release the arrested students and, more important, to refuse to sign the Versailles Treaty confirming new Japanese privileges in China. These events heightened nationalist sentiment within China. With Europe, Japan, and the United States discredited, many felt that China must seek national rejuvenation not in the West or in Japan, but within itself.

The loose unity of this intellectual or cultural revolution did not survive the mid-1920s. Its forces splintered into Marxist, liberal, and many other fragments. Nevertheless, the May Fourth Movement remained vivid as a demonstration of the new Chinese national spirit, and its message that the revolution must embrace more than political institutions continued to have a profound effect. The Kuomintang of Sun Yat-sen and his successors was never able to capture completely the support of all who were infected by the May Fourth Movement's ideas. The concept of a necessary revolution in values, behaviour, and attitudes remained free of association with any political party, its very independence reinforcing nationalistic demands for a new, proud, and free China.

Beginnings of Social Revolution

In the early years of the twentieth century, political and cultural upheaval was accompanied by changes in the traditional balance in the economic and social spheres. During the nineteenth century, western manufactured goods had found little demand in China, but at the beginning of this century they gradually began to have more and more effect on Chinese life. New, machine-made products competed with traditional handicraft products, and sometimes replaced them. For example, textile manufacture had been a traditional form of off-season employment for many peasant households, both for clothing the family and for extra income. Now, in a few regions, imported textiles could undercut the price of the native product. In many other areas, they could disrupt the demand for cheaper native goods by their superior quality and range of colour, or by capitalizing on the social fad in which foreign labels were considered more prestigious or modern. There is some debate among historians as to the extent of the penetration of imported western goods into the internal Chinese market, but there is little doubt that consumer demand was affected, particularly in the coastal cities and around the inland treaty ports.

Being "modern" involved transforming one's appearance and life-style to bring them more in line with what one thought of as "foreign." A Canadian missionary, born in China, commented on the changes he observed in these years:

> I was away from 1910 to 1912 . . . going away in 1910, we went away from an imperialist China that was advancing quite nicely. . . . But it was "Chinese" with still the long pigtail, the wide-sleeved coat and the high shoes with the thick felt soles for the mandarin. . . . Coming back, you had this craziest impact of western fashions which was what struck me as a young boy. For instance, the mark of a man was to have his pigtail cut off. Well, now, he didn't know how to cut it off. "Do you cut it off straight across?" . . . You had a variety of hairstyles that have never been equalled. Matter of fact, at the railway stations, there would be periodically queue cutters sent by the officials—China is going modern—particularly led by high school boys, radicals of the time. They would go along and without any ceremony and with pretty rough stuff, they would take a blunt pair of scissors and just cut across the pigtail where it was braided, cut it off

at the level of the coat collar. . . . Some went the whole hog, of course, and shaved their heads. That was both sanitary and it was modern too. Before that, a shaven head would represent either a person doing [religious] penance or a criminal, but now the shaven head became quite the thing —you were modern.

Two other things I remember. It was very modern to wear a felt fedora hat. These were made in China. There wasn't a good hat business, but they did their best, and they certainly put out a hodge-podge of fedora hats which you creased down the middle. The other mark of being an absolutely modern Chinese was to wear long winter underwear during the winter. But how would people know you had the underwear if you wore it inside? So they wore it outside. It was the craziest thing to see literally dozens of men, and these were the snobs of the city, who wore their long johns outside, and perhaps an umbrella in his hand—that also was a mark of status—and a felt fedora hat. This lasted for four or five years. . . .

. . . Also, for those few years, everything that was traditionally Chinese was looked down on and everything from the West was marvellous. The day of the dollar watch; the day of the flashlight coming in; the umbrella; the bicycle. . . . It became very swank to say a few words of English. The local turned-on fellow would be very happy, instead of bowing to you, to say "goodbye."[28]

These were superficial things, but in a traditional society of very sophisticated rules for social behaviour and social dress, they were outward signs of a much deeper questioning that was going on.

Foreign investment and the beginnings of industrialization in China affected the economy and the social structure far more than any previous western commercial contacts. In the early twentieth century, China was seen as a source of cheap labour. Foreign investors began opening factories in the treaty ports, not simply for the Chinese market, but also, under the protection of the treaties, for the processing of goods cheaply for export to other, more lucrative, foreign markets. Native Chinese industrialists kept step with the foreigners by opening factories to supply domestic demands, a trend which accelerated during 1914–18 when the Europeans were preoccupied with war at home.

Unchecked by government regulations, factories offered extremely low pay for long hours of work in abominable working conditions. Nevertheless, they provided an alternative to the traditional choice of work in the fields or in handicraft shops. Moreover, in the new factory's perspective of efficiency above all else, the adaptability of youth was a greater asset than the wisdom of the older generation. For all young people, the factory created job opportunities outside traditional family and community controls. For women, it offered perhaps even more revolutionary opportunities: for the first time, they began to play an important and even independent economic role. A married female factory worker could use her economic contribution to family finances as a lever to secure better treatment from her husband and his parents.

New social values also came about from broader educational opportunities. For centuries, the classical curriculum of the civil-service examination system had reinforced the traditional social values. After 1905, the examination system was gradually displaced by modernized government-supported schools on all levels. Missionary-sponsored schools multiplied, and private Chinese educational institutions sprang up. These new schools challenged the age-old concept that government service was the only legitimate purpose for education. They taught a curriculum more and more based on western concepts, and they introduced many ideas that conflicted with Chinese tradition—scientific progress, individualism, female education, social Darwinism, and nationalism, for instance. Specialization replaced the old, humanistic, non-specialist training of the traditional scholar-official. Students found a new bond as they were brought together in classes and larger school units instead of being isolated by the private tutoring they had received in homes or small local groups under the old system. Many thousands of graduates went abroad to Japan, Europe, and the U.S.A. for additional, specialized training. With the passing of the civil-service examination system went the traditional avenue of social advancement; in the early twentieth century, the new avenues were through business or military careers as well as government.

One must not assume that these changes penetrated all levels and all areas of China. The effects of economic and social changes were felt mainly within the cities, and the early twentieth century was marked by a growing separation of urban centres from the rural countryside. In traditional times, large cities had developed as administrative or commercial centres, but with strong links with their rural surroundings: government drew its principle tax revenue from the land; the society's dominant philosophy stressed the importance of the peasant-based economy; and the élite of the society were the rural-oriented gentry families. In the late nineteenth and early twentieth centuries, these links weakened. Commercial and industrial development began to transform the cities, but was not extensive enough to provide alternate employment for the average peasant household; and the peasant's income level remained too low to allow him to indulge in factory-made goods. Similarly, the new educational opportunities that existed within the urban centres were too distant and too costly for the average peasant's son or daughter even to contemplate. Thus the direct effects of industrialization were on city life; they did not create either new avenues for employment or a new life-style for the rural majority.

These urban transformations did, nevertheless, affect rural society in an indirect fashion. The peasant majority was immobile, but the gentry élite was not so restricted. Traditionally, the majority of gentry lived in local towns or smaller cities close to their landed holdings. In the late nineteenth and early twentieth centuries, the political disturbances of rebellions and warlord dominance added to the attraction of the cities' new amenities. Local gentry families began to move away from their ancestral homes to the larger urban centres. More and more, they left their lands in the hands of managing agents. Their new urban life-style tended to be costly, and resulted in additional demands on their tenants. Moreover, rents were now collected by an agent whose role was purely managerial and who was consequently less sensitive to traditional customs, such as an adjustment of rents during times of local economic difficulties.

Despite this hardening of traditional landlord-tenant relationships, tenancy grew as independent peasant cultivators increasingly found it difficult to survive. Landownership became concentrated in fewer hands, and peasant ownership became increasingly difficult to maintain. It is estimated that, during the 1930s, 53% of the cultivated land belonged to only 10% of the population, and some 40% of peasant farmers relied on borrowed food simply to live. Fully 30% of the land belonged to government officials and warlords, whose property escaped the tax rolls.[29] Thus the burden of taxes (in an age when government demands for more revenue were constantly expanding) fell upon the remaining 70% of the land. The results were evident in the declining living standard of the peasant populace and the rise in tenancy.

Thus, early-twentieth-century China experienced new social changes and new social tensions. In cities, particularly the great eastern-seaboard ports, new commercial and industrial activity created new opportunities, but also new forms of exploitation. In the rural areas, beset by growing population, civil warfare, and an apparent rise in absentee landlordism, the urban transformations meant little. For all the problems and brutality of lower-class urban life, the Chinese city-dweller could hope for better things, while life in rural China—the home of 80% of the people—continually deteriorated with little relief in sight. It is against this background that we must assess the history of the first half of the twentieth century.

Analysis

1. Nationalism is the main ingredient necessary for revolution. Consider this theory in relation to China in the early twentieth century, as well as any other revolution in the twentieth century.

2. No matter how much a revolution is expected, its actual occurrence is usually a surprise. Is this true of the 1911 revolution in China?

3. Assess the career of Sun Yat-sen as a revolutionary leader. To what extent does he represent the failure of liberalism in twentieth-century China?

4. If you were a revolutionary leader in China in the period of approximately 1890 to 1925, what situations, weaknesses, and changes would you take advantage of in order to achieve your end? Plan your strategy in specific ways in order to exploit each situation fully.

Suggested Readings

Shirley Garrett, *Social Reformers in Urban China: The Chinese YMCA, 1895–1926* (Cambridge: Harvard University Press, 1970).
  An interesting study of the social reform movement in these years, with the critical interaction between western and Chinese ideas and personalities.

Hsüeh Chün-tu, ed., *Revolutionary Leaders of Modern China* (London: Oxford University Press, 1971).
  Chapters 9–11 cover important Kuomintang figures other than Sun Yat-sen.

Pa Chin, *Family* (Garden City, N.Y.: Doubleday & Co., 1972).
  A novel first published in 1931 depicts well the social tensions of early-twentieth-century China as seen in the life of a family; written by one of the foremost progressive writers of the period.

Harold Z. Schiffrin, *Sun Yat-sen and the Origins of the Chinese Revolution* (Berkeley: University of California Press, 1968).
  The best study of Sun's career and ideas yet produced, although it does not proceed past 1905.

J. Spence, *The China Helpers: Western Advisers in China, 1620–1960* (London: The Bodley Head, 1969).
  Chapter 6 on Edward Hume deals with western educational influence in these years, and Chapter 7 is a very good short analysis of Mikhail Borodin, an extremely influential Comintern agent who aided Sun Yat-sen's reorganization of the KMT.

CHAPTER 11
The Nationalist Years, I

Chronology

1925 Death of Sun Yat-sen; May 30th incident in Shanghai.

1926 Chiang Kai-shek named Commander-in-Chief of KMT's Northern Expedition; Chiang's "mini-purge" of Communists in Canton region; Chiang launches Northern Expedition with c. 100 000 troops.

1927 Nanking captured and KMT forces clash with foreigners (March); Chiang launches "White Terror" purge of all CCP and leftists in Shanghai, followed by other southern cities (April); Chiang marries Soong Mei-ling, sister-in-law of Sun Yat-sen; Chiang ignores Wuhan KMT government and declares another Nationalist government at Nanking; Wuhan government collapses (September).

1931 Manchurian Incident leading to the establishment of the Japanese puppet state of "Manchukuo" under Henry P'u-i, the last Ch'ing emperor.

1931–4 Chiang's Bandit (i.e., Communist) Suppression Campaigns against Soviets in south and central provinces.

1934 New Life Movement organized under patronage of Madame Chiang Kai-shek.

1936 Sian Incident (December) and formation of Second United Front.

1937 Japanese invasion of north China (July 7); fall of Peking and Tientsin, and invasion of Shanghai (August); fall of Nanking (December).

1938 Japanese capture of Hankow (October); removal of KMT government to Chungking in Szechwan province (–1945).

1940 New Fourth Army incident (October).

1941 Japanese attack on Pearl Harbor, Hawaii (December 7/8).

1943 End to extraterritorial rights for foreigners in China.

1945 Japanese surrender after atomic bombing of Hiroshima and Nagasaki (August); battle between KMT and CCP troops for Manchuria begins (November); President Truman announces Marshall Mission (December); China receives Permanent Seat on Security Council of new United Nations.

1946 Political Consultative Conference (January); last Soviet troops evacuate Manchuria (March).

1947 KMT outlaws all minor political parties and purges the universities of all liberal elements.
1948 All Manchuria in Communist hands (November); beginning of strategic Hwai River battle for north China.
1949 CCP forces cross Yangtze (April); KMT government moves to Canton and then to Chungking; remnant KMT elements go with Chiang Kai-shek to Taiwan (December)

In 1927 the Kuomintang's Northern Expeditionary armies consolidated their new hold on the lower Yangtze basin and established a Nationalist government at Nanking. Between 1927 and 1949 the Nationalist government experienced a decade of relative stability, followed by eight long years of bitter struggle against Japanese invasion, and then by four years more of continuous civil war before it collapsed under the attacks of the Chinese Communists. In historical retrospect, these are hard years for the Chinese to assess dispassionately, and even more so for foreign observers. To some Chinese and foreigners, the eventual failure of the Kuomintang stemmed primarily from the perfidious aggression of Japan and the weak support given later by the United States for the KMT's brave struggle against Russian-inspired communism. To others, the failure resulted from the KMT's unholy alliance of traditionalism, militarism, and capitalism, finally giving way to the "natural revolutionary process" which embodied Chinese hopes for basic social change. For yet others, who see partial truth in each theory, the issue is more complex. One fact is patently clear: by 1949, most revolutionary nationalists were no longer willing to support the Kuomintang as the agent for a rejuvenated China. The progress of that disillusionment is our major concern in examining the Nationalist years.

Rupture of the United Front

Sun Yat-sen's dream of a reunified China seemed to be near realization shortly after his death in 1925. In early 1926 Chiang Kai-shek, Sun's protégé and superintendent of the Kuomintang's Whampoa Military Academy, was named Commander-in-Chief of the National People's Revolutionary Army, encompassing all the various Kuomintang forces. Shortly thereafter, the army left the Canton region and began the march north to unify the country.

Foreign antagonism to the Kuomintang's cause helped consolidate widespread sympathy for the Nationalists' Northern Expedition. Such sympathy was based in part on the memory of the May Fourth Movement and the general distrust of the West, which had grown over the years despite some western efforts to improve China's position. The Washington Conference of 1922 did result in Japan's withdrawal from the former German-leased territory in Shantung and in Britain's restoration of Weihaiwei to China. But the conference's stirring affirmation of the principles of the Open Door policy and of China's territorial integrity and administrative independence produced little practical result. An international conference in 1925–6 did agree to re-establish Chinese tariff autonomy by 1929, but a similar international meeting in Peking in 1929 failed to produce any agreement on extra-territorial rights—the other humiliating feature of the unequal treaty system. While there was some international good will, China obviously could not rely upon that alone. Nor was the weak, factionalized military government in Peking likely to speed the realization of China's nationalistic hopes.

Vastly outnumbered by the warlord armies if these had ever massed against them, the Nationalist troops profited from the divisions among the warlords. They were also aided by skilful propaganda teams who organized popular support well ahead of their advancing lines. The task of the propaganda teams was in turn greatly aided by the actions of the foreigners themselves. When British Concession police in Shanghai killed thirteen Chinese demonstrators on May 30, 1925, the incident sparked nation-wide protests. A similar occurrence in Canton in late June resulted in a fifteen-month strike in Hong Kong and a boycott of British goods throughout China. Chiang's Northern Expedition was launched in the midst of this aroused nationalism. By March 1927, Nationalist forces had secured the Yangtze region. In the following year, another campaign brought the northern provinces under the technical authority of the Kuomintang government, then located at Nanking.

The new Nanking government claimed legitimacy as heir to Sun Yat-sen's political philosophy. Since 1905, Sun had advocated a three-stage process for the republican revolution: the first was military government, dedicated to achieving national unification; the second was political tutelage, or the education of the Chinese people in the ways of constitutional republicanism while they remained under single-party rule; and the third was full constitutional government, in which the Kuomintang would transfer control to an elected parliamentary government. In 1927, in conformance with these ideas, the Nanking government formally declared the end of the first stage and the inauguration of political tutelage under the Kuomintang.

Political unification, however, remained more a hope than a reality. In reorganizing the Kuomintang in the early 1920s, Sun Yat-sen had brought together many diverse factions within the weak and divided revolutionary movement. The Kuomintang, however, despite attempts to emulate the example of the Russian Communist Party, never achieved internal party uniformity, and Sun's death removed the only real link between the disparate groups.

With Sun gone, a bitter debate on the meaning of the "revolution" quickly splintered Party ranks. An anti-Russian, conservative group split from the Party as early as 1925. In early 1926, a Kuomintang congress at Canton reaffirmed both Sun's policy of reliance on Russian aid and advisers and his tactics of incorporating Chinese Communist Party members within the Nationalist movement. But before launching the Northern Expedition, Chiang Kai-shek, on March 20, 1926, suddenly imprisoned all Chinese Communist Party members and Soviet advisers in the Canton region, claiming that their over-enthusiasm for social revolution challenged KMT authority and endangered the coming military campaign. He temporarily won his point, and he did this without splitting the Party, for both Soviet and Chinese Communists agreed upon the necessity of supporting Chiang temporarily and remaining within the Kuomintang. However, this shaky accommodation only postponed the real issue that divided Chiang and the Communists—whether social revolution would follow political unification.

The first major confrontation between Chiang and the Communists came in 1927. In mid-April, with Chiang's army approaching Shanghai, Communist-led agents and labour unions within the city prepared it for "liberation." Suddenly, the city was shaken by a bloody purge of all Communists and left-wing sympathizers. Depending on which version of the evidence one accepts, the purge was the work of either local anti-Communist organizations or Shanghai's underground criminal elements who had long-standing ties with Chiang Kai-shek. Similar bloody purges followed rapidly in various other southeastern cities recently captured by Chiang's forces.

On April 17, the Kuomintang's Central Committee, now at Wuhan and dominated by the left wing of the Party, responded by dismissing Chiang Kai-shek from his post as Commander-in-Chief. Chiang simply ignored the order and helped set up another government in Nanking, supported by the Party's right wing, the majority of the army, and the Chinese and foreign monied interests in the eastern-seaboard treaty ports. Chiang had, in effect, turned his back on social revolution. While, to many Chinese, social revolution was an essential element of the nationalist revolution, to Chiang and his supporters revolution meant political unification, international independence, and economic development, without further upset in the power structure of society.

The situation became further complicated in the summer of 1927, when a raid on the Russian embassy in Peking by agents of the collapsing Peking military government revealed documents that contained Moscow's secret orders to Russian advisers and their Chinese Communist allies to take over leadership of the Wuhan government. In response, the non-Communist progressives at Wuhan expelled both Russian and Chinese Communists and rejoined Chiang's Nanking government. The First United Front, created by Sun to unite all political forces for national revolution on behalf of all Chinese, thus dissolved in bloody confrontation at the moment of apparent military success in bringing unity to the country under one recognized government.

The Nanking Decade (1927–37)

In the subsequent decade Chiang Kai-shek became the undisputed symbol of Nationalist China. Born in 1886 into a family of landed gentry in Chekiang province on the south-central coastline, he received a classical education until the age of 18, when he enrolled in the Paoting Military Academy just outside Peking. In 1907 he attended a military academy in Japan, where he also joined Sun Yat-sen's exiled revolutionary group. He played only a minor military role in the Revolution of 1911, and shortly thereafter he disappeared into civilian life in Shanghai. During this obscure period, he apparently forged lasting connections with the political and financial interests of that city—both the legitimate native and foreign elements and the powerful underworld. In 1922 Chiang re-emerged as personal military assistant to Sun Yat-sen, and five years later he married Soong Mei-ling, sister of Sun Yat-sen's widow. Chiang adopted his wife's Methodist faith, and through her relatives he made valuable connections with American-educated Chinese (Madame Chiang was a graduate of Wellesley College in Massachusetts). All these threads—traditional educational values, military training, links with Sun's revolutionary heritage, association with Shanghai's political and financial establishments, and close ties with foreign-educated modernizers—were intertwined in his later career.

Consolidation of the new Nanking government's authority was an obsession with Chiang. His first priority was to deal with the persistent challenge of the Chinese Communists. Following the "White Terror," or purge, in the Kuomintang-held eastern cities in 1927–8, the Chinese Communists established several Russian-type soviets—tightly knit geographic units with independent political, economic, and military organizations—in rural regions in several south-central provinces. In response, Chiang's Nationalist army (with German advisers having replaced the Russians) mounted a series of massive military campaigns to isolate and gradually wipe out these soviets. Hammered and encircled, the Communists, in late 1934, abandoned their main southern bases and retreated to an isolated region in Shensi province in the northwest.

But the elimination of the direct Communist threat in the Yangtze heart of the new Nationalist regime was only one of Chiang's problems. Despite the apparent success of the Northern Expedition of 1926–8, four important military complexes and several lesser ones rivalled his government forces in the west and northwest, and while no rival government existed, Nanking's authority in these areas was purely nominal. Many warlords who "surrendered" in 1926–8 to the Northern Expedition (which obviously had the support of public opinion), continued to operate semi-independently, even while wearing Nationalist uniforms. Chiang Kai-shek constantly had to meet their challenge to full integration under the new Nanking government.

Thus, despite the optimistic declaration in 1927 of the transition from Sun Yat-sen's first stage of military reunification to the next stage of political tutelage, the goal of real unity escaped the Nanking government's grasp. Chiang Kai-shek kept trying to achieve full control, primarily by military means. Yet he did not succeed either in entirely eliminating the Communists or in subduing all other rivals. As one travelled beyond the lower Yangtze, main base of the KMT, real control by the Nationalist government faded rapidly.

Japanese Invasion and Civil War

Manchuria, in the extreme northeast, was one region that never came under Nanking's direct control. From 1911 to 1928 it was ruled by Chang Tso-lin (d. 1928), a warlord who, by using Japanese aid, countered Russian efforts to dominate the region. With Korea incorporated within their empire and extensive economic investments in the Manchurian region, the Japanese were uneasy about the prospect of a strong, unified, and nationalistic China. In 1928, when Chang Tso-lin hinted that he might support the new Nanking government, the Japanese arranged his assassination.

His son, Chang Hsüeh-liang, succeeded as Manchurian overlord after a brief power struggle with his father's other lieutenants. When the Young Marshal (as Chang was popularly known) raised the Nationalist flag over his Mukden headquarters, local Japanese army commanders took over direct control of the whole region in September

1931, without waiting for orders from their own high command, much less the Japanese government in Tokyo. After pushing Chang Hsüeh-liang's forces back south of the Great Wall into north China, the Japanese, changing the name of the region to Manchukuo, established a puppet regime under (Henry) P'u-i, the same Manchu emperor who had been ousted from the Chinese throne as an infant by the Revolution of 1911. Condemned as aggressors by the League of Nations, the Japanese withdrew from the organization and continued to hold onto this valuable territory in China.

Japan's imperialistic ambitions did not stop with Manchuria. Minor clashes between Japanese and Chinese troops south of the Wall produced a Nanking–Tokyo agreement in 1935, "neutralizing" the north China plain region. Still, agents of the Japanese Manchurian army (again frequently acting independently of their home government) continued to operate in the area. Their aim was to create a buffer state totally independent of Nanking and a protection for their Manchurian possessions. They were frustrated in these efforts by patriotic student protests, particularly in Peking, and by a Kuomintang-endorsed nation-wide boycott of Japanese goods. However, Chiang Kai-shek remained totally preoccupied with the Communist and warlord threats, and refused open confrontation with the Japanese, despite mounting popular demands for stronger resistance.

The Sian Incident of December 1936 marked the major turning-point in China's response to Japanese aggression. After losing Manchuria in 1931, Chang Hsüeh-liang had turned over his remaining troops to Chiang Kai-shek, while he himself went on a world cruise. On his return in 1935, he and his troops were shifted north to blockade the new Chinese Communist stronghold in Shensi province. In October 1936, Chang joined the growing list of those who demanded that Chiang Kai-shek lead a common effort against Japan. Chiang refused categorically, and on December 7 he flew to the Young Marshal's headquarters at Sian to discuss plans for a new anti-Communist campaign.

On his arrival in Sian, Chiang Kai-shek was arrested. The details of the next three weeks are not fully known. Ironically, it seems that

Chiang Kai-shek's life was saved by the intervention of the Chinese Communists, his bitterest enemies. Their agents had been in Sian for some time, fanning the desires of Chang Hsüeh-liang's troops to recover their lost Manchurian homeland rather than fight other Chinese. When Chiang was arrested, Chou En-lai and other leaders of the Chinese Communist Party arrived in Sian, endorsed the plea for a new United Front against the Japanese, and helped pressure Chiang Kai-shek into agreeing. On Christmas Day, the Kuomintang leader finally capitulated and was released. The details of the Sian arrangements were never openly announced, but the cessation of internal fighting was evident to the Japanese. The national hatred of foreign aggression had, for the time being, reunited China, even if its greatest national symbol, Chiang Kai-shek, had to be brought into the Second United Front by force.

A shooting incident on July 7, 1937, in a Peking suburb, during Japanese army manoeuvres near by, touched off full-scale conflict between China and Japan. From Manchuria, the Japanese launched a major invasion of north China. In mid-August, Shanghai was the target of a seaborne attack. Fighting between the Chinese and Japanese was fierce and bitter, but the superior mechanized equipment of the invading Japanese prevailed. The cutting of the Yellow River dikes by the retreating Chinese army stalled the Japanese northern campaign, though the inundation of the north China plain cost tens of thousands of lives as Chinese peasants were caught by surprise. By October 1938, the Japanese had taken Wuhan in the middle Yangtze and Canton in the southeast, and the basic battle lines for the next six years were established. The Nationalist government had withdrawn to Chungking, where, though harassed by Japanese air power, it was relatively safe behind the protecting hills of the upper Yangtze gorges. Chiang Kai-shek remained a national symbol, not of activism perhaps, but certainly of stubborn refusal to accept Japanese efforts at peace negotiations.

Chiang Kai-shek's wartime strategy was straightforward. Convinced that Japan must sooner or later collide with some other major power, he followed a policy of no-surrender and conservation of his own forces. The day after the Japanese attacked Pearl Harbor in Hawaii on December 7/8, 1941 (December 7 in the American time zone, December 8 in the Japanese), the United States declared war on Japan. Finally, Chiang Kai-shek had found his ally. It was not an easy association. Chiang's strategy, though static, demanded large-scale financial and material assistance, while the Americans, who wanted increased efficiency and aggressiveness on his part, were constantly frustrated in their hopes.

The Nationalist armed forces had been badly mauled in the original Japanese thrust into China, and, though rebuilt after the long retreat into southwest China, they proved very ineffective. Officers generally were chosen for their loyalty to Chiang Kai-shek rather than for their military skills. The few good officers found it difficult to succeed in a system governed more by political consideration than by strategic concerns. The average soldier was a badly treated, ill-fed, and ill-equipped conscripted peasant, with little desire to fight. The lack of enthusiasm was understandable. In describing the training camps for new recruits, one American newsman noted that "In some areas less than 20 per cent lived to reach the front."[30] The history of the war contains no great counter-offensive by Nationalist forces against the Japanese invaders.

One major reason lay in Chiang's main rivals, the Chinese Communists, who were technically his partners in the Second United Front. A central core of crack Nationalist troops were kept carefully in reserve or busy watching the Communist base in north-central China. The mounting stores of American aid, when not diverted by Nationalist generals and bureaucrats to the black market, were carefully hoarded for the future civil struggle that they foresaw at the end of the war. From their Shensi stronghold, the Chinese Communists pursued an active guerilla war extending well behind Japanese lines. Officially, under the United Front agreement of late 1936, the Kuomintang army command retained supreme authority over all anti-Japanese efforts. However, in October 1940 Nationalist troops attacked the Communists' New Fourth Army in the midst of a difficult retreat ordered by Kuomintang headquarters. Thereafter, the United

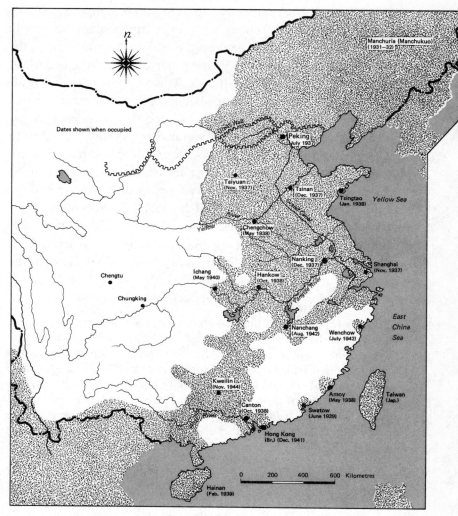

Map 9   Japanese-occupied Areas of China, 1937–45

Front was little more than a fiction. Communist representatives remained in Chungking, technically acting as a liaison between the CCP
and KMT war efforts, but the Communists conducted their own war
strategy and ignored any conflicting ''orders'' from Chungking.

Within Nationalist-held territory, demoralization at all levels characterized the later stages of the long war. Away from its familiar base in the commercial and industrial centres of the lower Yangtze valley, the government financed itself by pouring out ever-larger amounts of unbacked paper currency. Spiralling inflation and widespread profiteering by high government officials and political favourites effectively destroyed both the living standard and the confidence of the people. The general state of affairs frustrated every American effort to stimulate greater military activity and internal domestic reform. General Joseph W. Stilwell, a prickly American career officer, had learned to speak and read Chinese during duty tours in China dating back to 1921. From mid-February 1942 until his recall in November 1944, Stilwell was in charge of American co-ordination with Chinese and British forces against the Japanese offensive throughout southern Asia. He and Chiang Kai-shek had a never-ending battle of wills concerning American aid and the Chinese war effort. Stilwell's assessment of conditions in China was voiced in his diaries and papers:

> June 19 [1942] . . . The Chinese government is a structure based on fear and favor, in the hands of an ignorant, arbitrary, stubborn man. It is interlaced with family and financial ties and influences, which could easily tear it to pieces if pulled out. Faced with emergency, it has no alternative but to go on, and none of these interlocking interests predominate to the extent that any one of them could take over and clean house, even if the necessary patriotism were present, which it isn't. Only outside influence can do anything for China—either enemy action will smash her or some regenerative idea must be formed and put into effect at once.[31]

> January 19 [1943] . . . A gang of thugs with the one idea of perpetuating themselves and their machine. Money, influence, and position the only consideration of the leaders. Intrigue, double-crossing, lying reports. Hands out for anything they can get; their only idea to let someone else do the fighting; false propaganda on their "heroic struggle"; indifference of "leaders" to their men. Cowardice rampant, squeeze paramount, smuggling above duty, colossal ignorance and stupidity of staff, total inability to control factions and cliques, continued oppression of masses. The only factor that saves them is the dumb compliance of the *lao pai hsing* (the common people). The "intellectuals" and the rich send their precious brats to the (United) States, and the farmer boys go out and get killed—without

Uneasy alliance: General Joseph Stilwell, presenting Legion of Merit to Generalissimo Chiang Kai-shek at Chungking, July 1943.

care, training, or leadership. And we are maneuvered into a position of having to support this rotten regime and glorify its figure-head, the all-wise, great patriot and soldier — Peanut [Stilwell's favourite name for Chiang Kai-shek]. My God.[32]

[Undated] (I have) faith in Chinese soldiers and Chinese people: fundamentally great, democratic, misgoverned. No bars of caste or religion. . . . Honest, frugal, industrious, cheerful, independent, tolerant, friendly, courteous.

I judge Kuomintang and Kungchantang (Communist Party) by what I saw:

(KMT) Corruption, neglect, chaos, economy, taxes, words and deeds. Hoarding, black market, trading with the enemy.

Communist program . . . reduce taxes, rents, interest. Raise production, and standard of living. Participate in government. Practice what they preach.[33]

As the war dragged on, the Kuomintang stepped up its purges of liberal elements suspected of collaboration with the Communists. This was the state of things in China when American atomic bombs suddenly ended the war with Japan in August 1945.

The end of the war against foreign aggression immediately highlighted the differences between the Kuomintang and the Communists. To both parties, a confrontation between their conflicting ambitions for China was inevitable, despite both internal and external (particularly American) pressures on them, during and after the Japanese war, to settle their differences by political rather than military means. In August 1945 the Communists reiterated their terms, gaining strong support from the moderate liberal elements within the country. These terms sought an immediate end to "political tutelage," the Kuomintang's single-party dominance in the government, and Chiang Kai-shek's personal dictatorship. Chiang refused to be moved, putting his faith on apparently solid ground: the superior numbers and modern equipment of Nationalist forces, and the continuation of massive American aid.

The sudden peace left the Japanese occupation forces in China awaiting someone to accept their surrender. In the north, 53 000 American marines landed, occupying Tientsin and Peking and their surrounding mines and railways. Russia occupied the cities and communication links of Manchuria. The Chinese Nationalists were caught in remote southwestern parts of the country, but a large-scale American airlift flew these troops to the eastern seaboard. Chiang Kai-shek ordered the Chinese Communists to stand still, while Nationalist units moved northward to take over from the Americans and to accept surrender from the remaining Japanese forces. Throughout the north, Communist guerilla forces already controlled most of the rural countryside. The Communists bluntly rejected Chiang's orders, and in mid-November 1945, as Kuomintang troops tried to move into Manchuria, the final civil war between Nationalists and Communists began.

In early 1946, although compromised by their aid to the Nationalists, the United States tried to negotiate an agreement that would end the civil strife. As the special envoy of President Truman, General George C. Marshall managed to get smaller political groups, as well as the KMT and CCP, to convene a joint, multi-party conference. This Political Consultative Conference agreed on a formula for a coalition government, but its recommendations were stillborn. As Russian troops withdrew from Manchuria in early March, Chiang Kai-shek, interpreting Marshall's arranged truce as not applicable to Manchuria, airlifted Kuomintang troops to occupy all the major cities. Conflict with the Communist forces controlling the Manchurian countryside broke out immediately. Marshall's continued efforts were fruitless, and by mid-1946 full-scale civil war raged once again in the northeast.

The war lasted another three years. By autumn 1948, Communist forces controlled all Manchuria and had carried the offensive into north China, south of the Great Wall. From November 7 until the following January, the crucial battles were fought in the Hwai River valley, the gateway between the north China plain and the lower Yangtze basin. The Communists won a decisive victory, and when Chiang Kai-shek's plea for international intervention remained unanswered, he nominally resigned the presidency on January 21, 1949, one day before Peking (then called Peiping), the last Nationalist stronghold in north China, surrendered. Throughout the spring, as all the major cities in the lower Yangtze fell to Communist forces, Chiang managed to frustrate all efforts by other Kuomintang leaders to reach some compromise with the Communists. In June, he formally rejoined the Nationalist government, just before it fled once again to Szechwan. In December 1949, Chiang and the remnants of the Kuomintang flew to Taiwan. There they established a regime, with Chiang as President, which continued to claim sole legitimacy as the national government of all China.

Analysis

1. What are the arguments for and against the expulsion of the Chinese Communist Party from the Kuomintang in 1927?

or

Could Chiang have retained the CCP within the Kuomintang and still have achieved his objective of national unity?

2. What characteristics of Chiang helped him to maintain power from 1927 to 1949? To what extent can his methods be justified in light of the internal and external situation of the period? Account for his ultimate defeat.

Suggested Readings

Ch'ien Tuan-sheng, "The Kuomintang: Its Doctrine, Organization and Leadership," in A. Feuerwerker, ed., *Modern China* (Englewood Cliffs, N.J.: Prentice-Hall, 1964), 70–88.

    Drawn from the author's more detailed study, *The Government and Politics of China* (Cambridge: Harvard University Press, 1950), this very good summation covers the nature of the party from Sun Yat-sen's reorganization through Chiang Kai-shek's dominance.

J. Spence, *The China Helpers: Western Advisers in China, 1620–1960* (London: The Bodley Head, 1969).

    Chapter 9, "Chennault, Stilwell, Wedemeyer: A Compass for Shangri-La," deals with the three chief American representatives in China during the war years.

James C. Thomson, Jr., *While China Faced West: American Reforms in Nationalist China, 1928–1937* (Cambridge: Harvard University Press, 1969).

    A very good study on non-governmental relations between China and the U.S.A., containing excellent introductory and concluding chapters on the Nanking years.

CHAPTER 12
The Nationalist Years, II

Chronology (see pages 131–2)

Historical hindsight is never kind to losers, and the Nationalists are no exception. Perhaps the fairest approach to understanding their failure is to compare their actions with their espoused revolutionary ideals. As envisioned by Sun Yat-sen, the republican revolution was to result in government "of the people, by the people, and for the people." He envisioned a modern nation state that would foster both social justice and economic development, and that would finally break free of the humiliating legacies of the "century of shame." The Kuomintang saw itself as the legitimate heir of Sun's principles, and its record can be examined in their light.

Nationalism

The first of Sun's Three Principles of the People implied the dual task of achieving internal unification and resistance to imperialism. The Kuomintang regime did regain autonomy in the levying of tariffs. Internal administrative units such as Customs and the Post Office had their foreign personnel completely replaced by Chinese, many of them students returning from overseas with modern training. Foreign concessions shrank in numbers. New law codes and persistent diplomacy removed extra-territorial rights for citizens of minor powers, and in

1943, as a gesture to a wartime ally, Britain and the United States formally relinquished their rights of extra-territoriality, the last vestige of the old unequal treaty system. Following participation in certain prestigious wartime conferences, China was recognized as one of the five great powers with a permanent seat and veto rights in the Security Council of the new United Nations, which was formally founded at the San Francisco Conference of April 25–June 26, 1945.

Less impressive was the Kuomintang's record in achieving internal unity. In the face of the Communists and the remaining militarist rulers, Nanking had made some progress by the mid-1930s. However, after 1937 the Kuomintang regime moved westward, under the pressure of Japanese invasion, and became merely the "guest" of provincial military rulers, whose strength had never been completely broken. The Nationalists' lack of military activity during the long years between 1937 and 1945 increasingly marred their image as the focus of the people's hopes for a free China.

National unity had an inter-class, social dimension as well as a geographic definition, and here again the Kuomintang's record was less than impressive. In his lectures on the Three Principles, Sun had commented:

> The Chinese people have shown the greatest loyalty to family and clan with the result that in China there have been family-ism and clan-ism but no real nationalism. Foreign observers say that the Chinese are like a sheet of loose sand. Why? Simply because our people have shown loyalty to family and clan but not to nation—there has been no nationalism.[34]

To overcome this weakness in identifying with the Chinese nation, Sun did not seek to destroy the traditional identification with family and clan, but rather to build on it:

> [In the West] the individual expands immediately into the state; between the individual and the state there is no common, firm, social unit. So in welding the citizens together into a state, foreign countries do not have the advantage that China has. Because China lays emphasis upon the family as well as the individual . . . I think that in the relation between the citizens and their state, there must first be family loyalty, then clan loyalty, and finally national loyalty. Such a system, expanding step by step, will be

orderly and well regulated and the relationship between the small and large groups will be a real one.[35]

The Kuomintang inherited Sun's conservative attitude, emphasizing family ties as a stepping-stone to popular nationalism.

But the regime failed to stimulate a real sense of national feeling. Its failure stemmed from its inability to bring about a state system that would actively involve all elements of society. Chiang Kai-shek's Kuomintang distrusted social change, and built itself upon a narrow social spectrum. All projects to organize and assist the working classes or peasants were curbed unless they reinforced the regime's control. Except for some "paper" reforms—reforms passed but never implemented—the KMT abandoned the countryside to its traditional landlord and local militaristic control. With its revenue dependent on commerce and industry, and most of its personnel springing from the urban élite of the eastern seaboard, the Nationalists were psychologically and geographically separated from the bulk of the Chinese people.

Democracy or People's Rights

In 1929 the Nanking government formally announced the beginning of political tutelage, the second in Sun Yat-sen's three-stage program for republican revolution. Five branches of government were established, as set out in Sun's legacy. The first three—executive, legislative, and judicial—were obviously drawn from western, and particularly from American, examples. The last two—examination and control—were modernized versions of the traditional examination and censorial systems of imperial times (see pages 29–32). During political tutelage, all these branches were watched over and directed by a Council of State and a President selected by the Kuomintang, the only formal party allowed. Throughout the pre-1949 period, tutelage never really ended: the Party and the government remained intertwined at all levels. While the formal branches of government went through the motions assigned by their roles, effective power remained within the Kuomintang, and particularly in the hands of Chiang Kai-shek.

Despite reorganization in the early 1920s, the Kuomintang remained a coalition of factions rather than a coherent unit. After 1928 a self-perpetuating core, combining representatives of the army, the traditional rural élite, and the wealthy industrial and commercial urban elements, dominated the Party. Chiang's power rested on the strong personal loyalty of very diverse groups. His supporters included the army's officer corps, graduates of the Whampoa Academy, the "organization clique" which controlled many key offices in both Party and government, and, through his relatives by marriage, some western-trained economic experts. The Nationalist Party numbered somewhere between two and four million members, but it lacked the tight discipline and the commitment to common ends suggested by its structural resemblance to the Russian and Chinese Communist parties. Unlike western democracies, no concept of loyal opposition evolved either within or outside the Party, and contending cliques were united only through personal attachment to the leader.

Throughout the Nanking years and on into the wartime period, liberal elements both inside and outside the Kuomintang continued to hope for the eventual development of democratic procedures. A constitution was drafted in 1931, but it never became operative. A People's Political Council, containing representatives from many non-Kuomintang groups, was created in 1938. However, it remained ineffective because it had only advisory status and its advice was consistently ignored. In 1939, and again in 1945, "democratization" of local government was announced with great fanfare, but its main result was the reimposition of the ancient policing system of mutual responsibility and mutual surveillance. In November 1946, while the Manchurian civil fighting raged, the Nanking regime convened the long-promised National Assembly; but it was boycotted by liberal elements as well as by Communists because the dictatorship of the Kuomintang and Chiang Kai-shek remained intact.

The postwar conduct of the Nationalists alienated any remaining liberal sympathy for the regime. In September 1947 Washington's chief representative in China stated:

[There is] . . . the Kuomintang, whose reactionary leadership, repression and corruption have caused a loss of popular faith in the Government. . . .

Reactionary influences continue to mold important policies even though the Generalissimo [Chiang Kai-shek] remains the principal determinative force in the Government.[36]

Less kind observers had long before replaced the "even though" with "because." Corruption permeated the political administration and the military bureaucracy, frustrating reformers who were trying to work within the structure. The reoccupation of Japanese-held territories by the Kuomintang unleased an orgy of profiteering. Landlords demanded back rent and interest for the wartime years, while bureaucrats similarly tried to collect back taxes from people already bled dry by long years of Japanese occupation.

In 1947, all political groups other than those sponsored by the Kuomintang were outlawed. As well, many non-Party liberal intellectuals were hounded out of the educational system, out of suspicion and fear that their progressive views aided the Communists. Although repeatedly put down by force, Chinese university students staged protests against the tightening government control over intellectual life. As an American embassy official noted in early October 1947:

October 5/The student body in China plays such an important—and noisy—role in political life that I have been prowling around it here [in Nanking] to see what makes it tick. . . .

The University of Nanking is a classic example of the dilemma in which the Chinese intellectual finds himself today, to say nothing of the dilemma for anyone who would command his allegiance. By and large the Nanking student group still comes from the scholarly and the bureaucratic class despite the changes of the last century. Only a few come from humble origins or from the small emerging middle class. They instinctively think of themselves as the natural heirs of power. Generally they have liberal views, but liberalism to them means unrelenting opposition to the National Government and everything it does.

This opposition arises from Government failure to provide adequate financial support for education, while being only too willing to interfere in what the students and teachers consider to be purely academic matters. Both groups are bitter about the efforts to regiment them politically along Kuomintang lines. They supported the Kuomintang in its early revolutionary days when they had an important voice in its activities; now they are just told what to do and the penalties for failure to conform are often dreadful. They resent the failure, as they see it, to uphold the dignity and prestige of China. Thus, in the tradition of their fathers' student uprisings of a generation ago in support of the Kuomintang, they are as much nationalists as anything else.

. . . Actually the students seem convinced the Communists will be unable to take over, but that they can and will destroy the Kuomintang which will then permit the intellectuals to assume control. Anything which advances this aim is good; anything which hinders it is bad.

. . . They have little understanding of or interest in democracy or civil rights as we know them. Their goal is power for themselves, not the broadening of the base of power; and they assume that the future must be through state planning and some form of socialism, not capitalism or free enterprise—a view they share, incidentally, with the Kuomintang. In brief, the Government has lost the allegiance of the scholar class without which no government has long survived, and that allegiance is rapidly being thrown to the Communists.[37]

Increasingly fearful and suspicious, the Kuomintang regime defined patriotism as loyalty to the Nationalist Party and to its leader; any other position was construed as support for the enemy. Ostensibly tutoring the Chinese people toward eventual democratic republicanism, the Nationalists patently blocked any real progress toward that end.

People's Livelihood

As expressed by Sun in the early 1920s, the principle of People's Livelihood outlined, only in a very general way, a policy of "national reconstruction" that was to follow the achievement of national unity. It included, in the vaguest of terms, the gradual redistribution of land to those who worked it. Industrial development was to be encouraged, with capital investments regulated by the government, which would also own the principal enterprises. The Marxist concept of class struggle as the means to achieve social justice was expressly rejected as inappropriate to Chinese experience and tradition. Sun proposed instead that workers and peasants be protected by active government control of the economy. He also welcomed foreign capital with which to build up an industrial base.

The Kuomintang did achieve some significant advances. Before the

Japanese invasion cut short the Nanking years, the recovery of tariff autonomy to some extent protected infant native industries against foreign competitors. Road and rail transportation networks were expanded and air transport introduced. A new unified dollar currency brought order to a monetary system that had been chaotic since at least 1911. A procedure for government budgeting was inaugurated, the heavy load of interest and capital repayments on foreign debts was met, and government banks regained the initiative from foreign financial institutions in large-scale domestic monetary transactions. In blueprint, the social and economic legislation of these years covered every area of life from footbinding to rural credit.

On the other hand, there were serious blots on the Nationalists' record. While revisions in the tax structure provided for a centralized system and made collection more efficient, no equitable scale of taxation evolved. The Kuomintang was unwilling or unable to levy a progressive income tax on upper-income groups. Furthermore, in 1928 the central government had decided to abstain from taxation of the rural sector. This decision reflected both the government's lack of control in most of rural China, and also the social composition of the Kuomintang, the majority of which came from landowning families. Rural and provincial taxation was abandoned to the caprice of provincial authorities. Central government revenue came mainly from the modern sector of the economy, some eighty-five per cent of tax income being raised by indirect taxes on foreign trade and industrial production.

Lack of revenue was compounded by the narrowness of Kuomintang financial policies. Despite budgeting, government revenues were eaten up by the huge military establishment, and none found their way into any sustained economic or social program. Government intervention and involvement in modern industrial development dated from the late nineteenth century, and Sun Yat-sen's ideas further justified this practice in terms of protecting the people's livelihood. In Kuomintang hands, however, government control of investment became the means of concentrating wealth and power in the hands of a small circle of powerful government officials and supporters, including Chiang

Kai-shek's own relatives by marriage. This group used its political position and influence to create massive private holdings in industry and finance. As one student of the period noted:

> The economic literature of the Nanking period, much of it written by the government élite, is replete with justifications for this version of the "controlled economy." . . . Through a variety of screened manoeuvres, however, industries which the government had transferred to its ownership, began to gravitate into the private control of important members of the Kuomintang elite. Under the guise of Sun's principle, a small but powerful group of government officials came to dominate much of China's modern industry and banking resources as private business magnates.[38]

Private enterprises found little incentive to expand, and foreign capital investment virtually halted. Sun Yat-sen's concept of controlled enterprise in the interests of both development and social justice was perverted into a system that became known as "bureaucratic capitalism." The result of this type of economic policy was assessed by one scholar in the following manner:

> In summary, then, because of the priority given national unification by force, the Nationalist government was unable to affect economic development to any great extent through its own spending policies. It was not able to draw excess capital from the land because of its "hands-off" land tax policy, and its policy of basing tax revenue on the modern sector of the economy tended to hamper the development of the private sector. Bureaucratic capitalism had a further pernicious effect on the private sector. In the Nanking period there was thus little or no development in the public sector, and only limited development in the private sector. Nor was the private sector controlled so as to benefit the many as Sun Yat-sen had hoped. The result was a general picture of economic stagnation.[39]

During the war and in the postwar years, this tolerable if shaky economic situation rapidly deteriorated. Financing by issuing more paper money, rather than by effecting tax reform, fuelled an inflationary spiral which, by late 1948, had raised the average price level to 6 250 000 times the prewar figures![40] Savings and investment were destroyed, salaries became meaningless, and the basic livelihood of worker and peasant was undermined.

These stark contrasts with the revolutionary aims of Sun Yat-sen's Three Principles reflect a poverty of new ideas within government circles in the Nationalist era of political power. Few theories and plans of non-Party intellectuals found their way into government thinking, and the more progressive people within the Kuomintang never wielded much influence. The piecemeal reform legislation that was enacted was not fully enforced. The poverty of ideas was also evident within the country's educational system, especially during the wartime years. Memorization and the recitation of facts were the order of the day, interspersed with heavy doses of the Kuomintang interpretation of Sun's Three Principles.

Conservative nationalism was the key feature of Kuomintang ideology. Under Chiang's influence, it emerged as a curious mixture of old Chinese and modern western ideas. Western modernism was particularly adopted in the field of finance, but even here, elaborate schemes of economic development were divorced from the reality of the country's backward economy and were doomed from the start by the heavy hand of bureaucratic capitalism. The high-placed framers of these schemes often identified personal wealth with national wealth, just as they identified their own continued control with national political power. Militarism was an inseparable part of Kuomintang rule. This was reflected in the enormous financial cost of its continuous dedication to military strength as the prime method for achieving national unity.

In a revival of Self-Strengthening efforts to blend modern technology with traditional moral values, the KMT based its modern approaches to high finance, political-party structure, and military might on very conservative, traditional values. The New Life Movement was launched in the 1930s under Madame Chiang's patronage. As well as being anti-Communist, it espoused unity, discipline, physical fitness, cleanliness, and orderliness, all set forth philosophically in terms of the Confucian virtues of propriety, integrity, and a sense of shame.

After 1945, public confidence in the KMT melted away. Neither peasant nor industrialist benefited from its mixture of western capitalism and Chinese bureaucracy. Advocates of liberal democratic principles were no more pleased with the Kuomintang's record than were left-wing, revolutionary activists. And despite elaborate government propaganda, the disparity between proclaimed high moral values and the conduct of many KMT officials created increasing public disillusionment. In the eyes of many, the KMT's conservative nationalism seemed less a force for national rejuvenation than a protective shield for a privileged and largely parasitic élite. When renewed civil war broke out, the majority of Chinese people (who could remember very few years of peace within their lifetime) were content to watch from the sidelines in the belief that nothing could be worse than their past experience.

Analysis

1. Were Sun's Three Principles the answer to the basic problems facing China? Why?
2. Why did Chiang not completely apply the Three Principles?
3. To what extent was Chiang's rule a fascist form of government? Compare his government to either Hitler's or Mussolini's government in the 1930s.
4. Chiang's rule represented a necessary transitional phase from Manchu to Communist rule. Discuss.

Suggested Readings

Pichon P.Y. Loh, *The Kuomintang Debacle of 1949: Conquest or Collapse?* (Boston: Heath, 1965).
   A judicious selection of readings on the reasons for KMT failure, incorporating a variety of views.
John Melby, *The Mandate of Heaven: Record of a Civil War, China 1945-49* (Toronto: University of Toronto Press, 1968).
   A very useful, as well as interesting, diary of a former American diplomat in China, covering the period from 1945 to 1949.
Mary C. Wright, *The Last Stand of Chinese Conservatism* (Stanford, Calif.: Stanford University Press, 1957).

This study, a detailed examination of the T'ung-chih restoration of 1862-74, includes on pages 300-12 a comparison of the ideological similarities between Chiang Kai-shek and the nineteenth-century Self-Strengtheners. This is a more readily accessible source for the same author's more detailed study on "From Revolution to Restoration: The Transformation of Kuomintang Ideology," *Far Eastern Quarterly*, XIV, No. 4 (August, 1955).

SECTION III SUMMARY AND RESEARCH

1. The author entitled Section III "The Search for Respectability." Do you think this is a reasonable choice? Why?
2. Read the sections of *The Stilwell Papers* which deal with Chiang. What do they reveal about Chiang as a person? as a leader?
3. Considering his supporters, his beliefs, and his personality, there was no way that Chiang could have created an effective strategy to win the civil war. Is this a valid hypothesis? Explain your view.

SECTION IV
THE NEW CHINA

CHAPTER 13
The Stubborn Alternative

Chronology
1917 Bolshevik Revolution in Russia.
1918 Ch'en Tu-hsiu and Li Ta-chao form first Marxist study group.
1920 Arrival of first Comintern agent in China.
1921 Founding Congress of the Chinese Communist Party (July 1) held secretly at girls' boarding-school in Shanghai French Concession.
1927 Mao Tse-tung's "Report on an Investigation of the Hunan Peasant Movement" (February 27); rupture of First United Front, and Chiang Kai-shek's purge of Communists from KMT.
1928–34 Establishment of Chinese soviets and fight to preserve them against Nationalist attacks.
1934–5 Long March from Kiangsi Soviet to Yenan.
1935–49 The Yenan years.

The Russian Revolution of 1917 coincided with the intellectual and political ferment associated with the May Fourth Movement. To the Chinese, the Russian experience demonstrated that one need not reach back to the French or American revolutions for a model of rapid change. Later, both the political philosophy of Marx, on which the Russian Revolution was based, and the techniques of organization advocated by Lenin made a strong impact on Chinese revolutionary thought and action. A look at these two European personalities who left such a deep mark on modern China is therefore necessary.

Karl Marx (1818–83), a German by birth, witnessed the rapid spread of industrialization in Europe. In the advanced industrial nations of his day he was struck by the misery of the working classes, which he blamed on the capitalist owners of the means of production. He concluded that only violent revolution and the full restructuring of society could fundamentally improve conditions for the workers. He set out to place these observations within a theoretical framework which, he hoped, would have universal validity because it would be based on "scientific laws" of human society. From these "laws" it would be possible to deduce concrete courses of action to change society.

His belief in the inevitability of working-class revolution stemmed from his examination of history. To Marx, history was a process in which societies passed through various stages of economic organization: from primitive communalism through slavery to feudalism and finally into the bourgeois capitalist system. In all societies in which a system of ownership prevailed, there were class divisions and a class struggle between the owners of the means of production and the exploited labourers. These struggles were responsible for historical change and progression.

Convinced that he had constructed a scientific theory of history and social change, Marx forecast humanity's future in an industrial society. A proletarian, or working-class, revolution against the capitalist exploiters would initiate an intermediate socialist stage in the transformation of society. In this phase, the state would serve the interests of the working masses by wresting the power of government and the economic means of production from the control of the bourgeois minority. Once this process was completed, the elimination of private ownership would result in the evaporation of class distinctions. Without class interests, and hence without class conflict, the final stage of the true communist society would provide peace, international order, social justice, and economic security for all.

Marxism's revolutionary potential was seized and harnessed in the early years of this century by Vladimir Ilych Ulianov (1870–1924), better known as Lenin, and by his fellow Bolsheviks. Lenin insisted that a successful revolution required leadership by a cohesive core of professional revolutionaries, bound together tightly in a party organization. This "democratic centralism" included a party structure based on local cells, or groups, of individual party members. Elected delegates from the local groups attended higher congresses, which in turn elected their own executive committees. At the top of the pyramid of congresses stood the national party congress and the central executive committee, whose standing committee exercised day-to-day administrative power over the whole structure. The system was called "democratic" because of the elective process which reached up from the bottom; "centralism" implied that the higher the level, the greater and broader the authority in decision-making. Ultimately, the supreme power of the standing committee of the central executive committee extended down to the lowest level. The Russian Revolution of 1917 was a testing ground for these theories, as well as for Lenin's single-minded leadership. Its success powerfully affected all aspiring revolutionary movements thereafter.

Lenin's political theory and his intellectual sophistication enhanced his appeal to non-western intellectuals. In particular, they were deeply interested in his "scientific" explanation of western imperialism, which was based on Marxist theories. Lenin saw imperialism as the inevitable product of western capitalism, as countries competed and fought for new markets and new sources of raw materials. Imperialism, however, was the last stage of exploitive capitalism, and would cease to exist when capitalism was overthrown and replaced by socialism and communism. Thus the proletarian revolution, in the name of the international brotherhood of all working peoples, would end imperialist exploitation. Lenin's revolutionary theories and techniques had an enormous influence on early-twentieth-century Chinese intellectuals who were seeking both ideas and means whereby to create a new China.

The Early Chinese Communist Party (CCP)

In September 1918, two Peking University faculty members, Ch'en Tu-hsiu (1880–1939), Dean of Letters, and Li Ta-chao (1888–1927), University Librarian, founded a society for the study of Marxism. Both were prominent figures in the intellectual revolution then in progress (see pages 122–4). Ch'en in particular was well known as editor of *The New Youth*, the popular journal through which the ideas of "Mr. Science" and "Mr. Democracy" were propagated. In February 1920 Gregory Voitinsky, an agent of the Communist International, or Comintern, arrived in Peking. He was the first visible symbol of Soviet Russia's interest in China's revolutionary prospects. Much of the subsequent history of communism in China reflects the interaction of these two strands: Chinese interest in Marxism–Leninism's applicability to the Chinese revolution; and Russian interest in stimulating socialist revolutions along the lines of its own experience.

Founded at a secret meeting in the Shanghai French Concession in early July 1921, the infant Chinese Communist Party numbered some fifty members. Among them was Mao Tse-tung (1894–1976), a former library assistant to Li Ta-chao at Peking University, who served as secretary to the Party's founding congress. The Shanghai assembly adopted the Leninist party structure. It also shifted the emphasis of its members' activities from the intellectual study of Marxist theory to the organization of Chinese urban workers.

When Russian advisers to Sun Yat-sen helped reorganize the Kuomintang in 1924, CCP members reluctantly accepted the Comintern policy of a "united front". Such a policy followed Lenin's concept of appropriate revolutionary tactics in countries that lacked sufficient internal economic development to sustain an independent proletarian movement. Since China had only a minuscule industrial proletariat, the Russians advised the Chinese Communist Party members, as individuals, to join the larger nationalistic revolutionary movement under the direction of the Kuomintang. The Comintern reasoned that the multi-class nationalistic movement, with Communists and workers as part of it, would increase revolutionary tendencies among the people, and this would hasten the time when the representatives of the proletariat (i.e., the Communists) could grasp leadership from within the larger, bourgeois-led movement headed by Sun Yat-sen.

Initially, this tactic seemed to work well. By early 1925, CCP membership had grown to almost a thousand. The Communists' energy and skill in organizing labour unions and peasant groups for political action gave them a decided advantage over their KMT allies. Several Communists held key posts within the Kuomintang itself. For example, Mao Tse-tung, though still a minor figure within the CCP, was an alternate member of the Kuomintang's Central Executive Committee, and ran a training centre in Canton for KMT organizers of peasant movements. He rose to be secretary and finally deputy head of the Kuomintang's Propaganda Department. It was against such successes by Communists and left-wing sympathizers that Chiang Kai-shek took action in 1926–8.

Even in the midst of Chiang's brutal purges in the eastern provinces, the Comintern ordered the CCP to remain united with the left-wing KMT government at Wuhan, until it collapsed in September 1927 (see pages 134–5). By January 1928, within the territories controlled by Chiang's Nanking government, all CCP members and their allies were either in jail, or in hiding, or dead. Those who escaped Chiang's net attempted to counter-attack by organizing armed uprisings in several southern cities, but these were crushed quickly by the expanding power of Chiang's Nationalist troops.

Driven from the cities, the revolutionary activity of the CCP switched to the rural regions where several soviets were organized as bases from which to recapture the urban centres. The most famous of these was formed at Ching-kang-shan on the Hunan–Kiangsi border. Here, Chu Teh (1886–1976) brought the small number of Communist troops which were formerly part of the Kuomintang's Northern Expeditionary Force, and used them as a nucleus for the building of the Red Army. He joined Mao Tse-tung and others who were already there, organizing the administrative structure of the soviet. Together they made the Kiangsi Soviet into a model of a "rural base area" — a self-contained and self-sufficient region conducting guerilla warfare against the Nationalists.

Chiang Kai-shek's forces attacked the various Communist soviets in successive "bandit-suppression" campaigns (so labelled to recall traditional government action against any challenging domestic force). The Kiangsi Soviet was under great pressure. It was indicative of the future independence of the CCP that, by the time Comintern orders arrived to abandon Kiangsi, the local Chinese Communist leaders, on their own authority, had evacuated it two weeks before. In October 1934, the Long March began.

It was during these tumultuous years in the Chinese revolutionary movement that Mao Tse-tung first differed with Moscow doctrine. Unlike Chiang Kai-shek, Mao was born in a peasant environment and knew at first hand the hard life of the peasant majority. In early 1927 he wrote a report based on two years of activity in organizing peasant movements in the familiar rural areas of his home province of Hunan in central China. In this report, Mao broke with the European Marxist concept that an exploited industrial proletariat was the essential element in bringing about revolution. (The italicized sentences are underlined in the original.)

> Within a short time, hundreds of millions of peasants will rise in Central, South, and North China, with the fury of a hurricane; no power, however strong, can restrain them. They will break all the shackles that bind them and rush towards the road of liberation. *All imperialists, warlords, corrupt officials, and bad gentry will meet their doom at the hands of the peasants.* All revolutionary parties and comrades will be judged by them. *Are we to get in front of them and lead them or criticize them behind their backs or fight them from the opposite camp?*[41]

The Chinese Communist Party, then, should lead the rebellious peasantry, the time-honoured force for change in China. The peasants, rising against gentry landlordism (what Mao called "rural feudal power"), and not the urban workers against bourgeois capitalism, should become the major revolutionary focus.

For those within the CCP who might not be prepared for the realities of peasant uprisings, Mao had some words of warning:

> . . . a revolution is not a dinner party, or writing an essay, or painting a picture, or doing embroidery; it cannot be so refined, so leisurely and gentle, so temperate, kind, courteous, restrained and magnanimous. A revolution is an insurrection, an act of violence by which one class overthrows another. A rural revolution is a revolution by which the peasantry overthrows the power of the feudal landlord class. Without using the greatest force, the peasants cannot possibly overthrow the deep-rooted

authority of the landlords which has lasted for thousands of years. The rural areas need a mighty revolutionary upsurge, for it alone can rouse the people in their millions to become a powerful force. . . . To put it bluntly, it is necessary to create terror for a while in every rural area, or otherwise it would be impossible to suppress the activities of the counter-revolutionaries in the countryside or overthrow the authority of the gentry. Proper limits have to be exceeded in order to right a wrong, or else the wrong cannot be righted.[42]

The house at Shao-shan, Hunan, where Mao Tse-tung was born in 1893, is now a famous national site and attracts many tourists, both Chinese and foreign.

Mao's roots in the rural countryside dictated his approach to the revolution as a peasant upheaval. Moreover, personal experience had already hardened him against the academic, textbook type of revolutionary who was far removed from the suffering masses.

Chiang Kai-shek's violent purge of the Communists from the cities and the experience of the Kiangsi Soviet persuaded Mao to speak up. He pressured Party leaders to make Marxism–Leninism more relevant to the Chinese situation by putting the CCP at the head of the peasantry, by far the largest class in China. However, Communist leadership was still dominated by urban intellectuals like Ch'en Tu-hsiu, who followed Moscow's more orthodox view that rural soviets were simply temporary expedients, staging areas from which to re-establish the revolution on the proper base of the industrial proletariat. But by the early 1930s, only the rural soviet movement retained any vitality as a revolutionary core, and its chief organizers included Mao Tse-tung and his allies, who believed in a Chinese form of revolution based on the peasant class.

The Long March and the Yenan Years

The Long March, celebrated in song, dance, and film, marked a significant dividing line in the fortunes of the Chinese Communist revolutionary movement. Of the total CCP forces, roughly 100 000 men were based at the Kiangsi Soviet. They began the trek from Kiangsi, on October 16, 1934, to escape Chiang Kai-shek's forces. Over a year was spent on a long, circuitous route (see Map 10), traversing nearly 10 000 kilometres of rivers, mountain ranges, and mudflat grasslands. Fighting punctuated the entire march. Sometimes the attack came from Chiang's troops, sometimes from remnant war-lords, and sometimes from hostile local tribesmen. Of the original marchers, only 8 000 were left in the weary columns that finally came to a halt at Yenan, in northern Shensi province. A drab market town, Yenan's sparse population and poverty were a far cry from the CCP's earlier base in the bustling cities of the southeastern seaboard. When stragglers filed in from other soviets to join the survivors of the Long March, the Communist fighting forces still only totalled roughly 50 000 men, a small percentage of their earlier strength. Yet from this seeming disaster came the lessons, the heroic image of sacrifice, and the revolutionary determination to persevere, which ultimately carried the movement to success.

An important party conference was held in the middle of the Long March. This conference set Yenan as the final destination and elected Mao Tse-tung as Chairman of the Politburo, the chief policy-making body within Communist Party structure. This marked the eclipse of the power of the Moscow-oriented faction within the CCP. Mao's election gave new force and direction to the movement. As one scholar expressed it: "Apart from being a personal triumph, his election to such an important post represented a victory of the rural soviet over the urban party centre, of a man who had spent all his life among the peasants and the lower orders of society over those who were well-versed in doctrines, Eastern and Western."[43]

Mao had lost a younger sister and a wife in the Kuomintang's anti-Communist campaigns, and he had personally endured the Long March, during which many close friends as well as a younger brother and two children had died. Despite all this, in the Long March experiences Mao saw the indomitable spirit of the revolution:

> The Long March is also a manifesto. It proclaims to the world that the Red Army is an army of heroes and that the imperialists and their jackals, Chiang Kai-shek and his like, are perfect nonentities. It announces the bankruptcy of the encirclement, pursuit, obstruction and interception attempted by the imperialists and Chiang Kai-shek. The Long March is also an agitation corps. It declares to the approximately two hundred million people of eleven provinces [traversed en route] that only the road of the Red Army leads to their liberation. Without the Long March, how could the broad masses have known so quickly that there are such great ideas in the world as are upheld by the Red Army? The Long March is also a seeding-machine. It has sown many seeds in eleven provinces, which will sprout, grow leaves, blossom into flowers, bear fruit and yield a crop in future. To sum up, the Long March ended with our victory and the enemy's defeat.[44]

At the time of this statement, in December 1935, these words might have been dismissed as mere rhetoric, but there is no doubt that the Long March and Mao's leadership infused a new and vibrant energy into the CCP.

The choice of Yenan also had a profound effect on the fortunes of the Communist movement in China. Yenan was selected as a remote refuge from Kuomintang harassment, but it had additional advantages. As communication with the outside was limited, the CCP's new nerve centre was free of the heavy directing hand of Moscow. Also, the surrounding area was poverty-stricken, so the Communists had to develop an immediate economic program to win over the local peasantry and make it possible for the region to support the increased burden of the Party's administrative and military personnel. Finally, Yenan placed the Party close to the front line of the coming war against Japan.

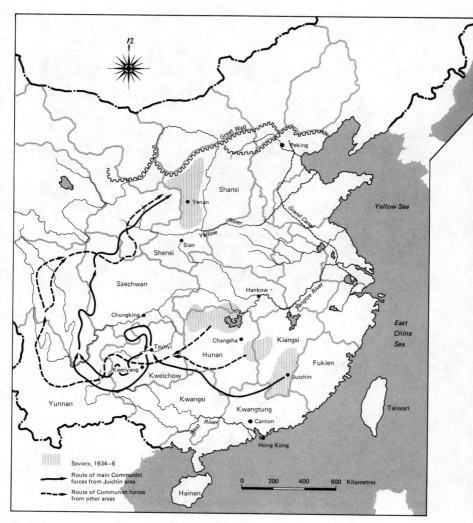

Map 10   The Long March, 1934–5

Each of these factors contributed to the CCP's revival.

When the Japanese invaders came in 1937, they took control, as the Kuomintang had done, mainly of the coastal cities and the interlinking

People's Liberation Army troops along the Great Wall during the anti-Japanese war (1937–45).

road and railway networks. The Communists had learned from their guerilla experience in the earlier soviets to concentrate their efforts in the rural areas, which contained the vastly greater proportion of both land and people. The Japanese occupation resulted in the wholesale flight from occupied territories of the landlord gentry and the local officials allied to the Nationalist regime. Those who remained were powerless to resist Communist pressures for change. And, as the Japanese occupation troops made forays from their urban bases, their brutality aroused the wrath of the peasants and made them willing recruits for Communist-led partisan groups.

While the Kuomintang spent the wartime years digging in and protecting its southwestern bastion, the Chinese Communists expanded throughout the north and central regions well behind Japanese lines. Their organizational skills and guerilla strategies enabled them to mobilize the anti-Japanese sentiments of the people. Oppressed for centuries by imperial governments and warlord regimes, and neglected by the Nationalists, the Chinese peasants now had their first real champions since the Taiping Rebellion.

The anti-Japanese war effort was only one part of the Communist plan. The other major objective was to make a united people out of the masses of peasants in the areas under Communist control. In contrast to the Nationalists, the Yenan Communists implemented an active program of socio-economic change. In the earlier period of the soviets, outright confiscation of property and violent elimination of the gentry class had characterized the revolutionary administration. By comparison, the Yenan period seemed a retreat from such drastic social policies. Expropriation and land redistribution were continued in cases of landlords who had either fled with the Kuomintang or collaborated with the Japanese. Otherwise, rents were simply restricted to no more than one-third of the crop, and interest payments on loans to peasants were lowered. This more moderate policy made it possible for gentry and rich peasants remaining in Communist territory to support the CCP's anti-Japanese activities. These gentry, however, did lose their special privileges: in Communist territories the gentry's dominant social and political position was usurped by Communist representatives, backed if necessary by the authority of the Red Army.

Although the Nationalist government was the only official, formal government in China, the CCP territories operated under their own alternative political structure. Certain territorial bases, radiating from Yenan eastward to the coast and down through the lower Yangtze, were designated as "liberated areas." Although tied to the central authority at Yenan, each of these areas also possessed separate political structures enabling them to operate efficiently on their own. Their territories largely ignored the lines of the Japanese occupation, incorporating large areas of rural China well behind the enemy's front lines. Numbering nineteen by 1945, these liberated areas contained some ninety million Chinese, organized into separate regional units under Communist control.

By the end of the war, CCP membership stood at about a million and a half, and Party workers were spread throughout the population, living and working with the peasants and acting as military and political leaders. Government positions at all levels (except in the highest policy-making bodies) were open to sympathetic non-Party activists. Mass organizations encouraged peasant interest and participation in village meetings, peasant associations, women's leagues, mutual-aid teams, and co-operatives. The Communists wanted everyone actively involved in the revolution, and no area, village, or person was overlooked.

The military power of the Communists included numerous village militia and guerilla forces, capped by regular forces, namely the Red Army. In the Red Army, the Chinese peasant met a new type of military organization. Like the local guerilla bands and militia, the Red Army was a volunteer force. Traditionally, the Chinese had looked down on soldiering as an inferior, rough occupation, and the common people had become hardened in their negative attitude toward the military by the experiences of the warlord years. The Communist areas witnessed a startling change in this traditional attitude.

Constant indoctrination campaigns within the Red Army heightened morale and strengthened discipline within its ranks. Impartial military justice ensured conformance to the image of a Communist soldier, as set down in Mao's stern injunctions:

1. speak politely
2. pay fairly for what you buy
3. return anything you borrow
4. pay for anything you damage
5. don't strike or swear at people
6. don't damage crops
7. don't take liberties with women
8. don't ill-treat captives.[45]

In themselves, these simple rules indicate the kind of brutal behaviour that the peasants formerly expected of anyone in military uniform, and therefore the Communist forces' adherence to these rules dramatically affected popular attitudes toward them. In contrast with army service in the past, being a soldier in a Communist force became a proud occupation.

Its rigorous code of conduct and its ideal of serving the people were reinforced by the Red Army's varied roles outside strictly military activities. Everywhere, but particularly in regions close to the Japanese, Red Army soldiers acted as local administrators, carried out land reform, opened schools and medical clinics, and provided a reserve labour corps for such tasks as planting and harvesting. The Red Army was not only a fighting force, but also an agency for the revolutionary aims of the Communist movement.

These years marked the full emergence of Mao Tse-tung as the Party's leading thinker. Early in his life he had developed a strong hatred of imperialism, a profound conviction of the revolutionary potential of the common people, and an unshakable faith in "voluntarism," or the unlimited capacity of men and women who are fired with revolutionary fervour. During a short stay in Peking at the height of the May Fourth Movement, the young Mao was attracted to Marxism–Leninism. But his active involvement in the events of his day meant that he had little time to work out a coherent political philosophy. The Yenan years provided that opportunity, with the Chinese Communists now based in the countryside and free of Russia's control over ideological orthodoxy. During this period, the mature Mao incorporated his practical experiences within the framework of the Marxist explanation of history. The result was a new, sophisticated doctrine of socialist revolution in the Chinese context.

Mao reworked the concepts of class and party that were so important in Marxist–Leninist doctrine. While he remained orthodox in his dedication to a socialist revolution of the proletariat, the definition of "proletariat" subtly changed — revolutionary commitment rather than class origin became the essential element, and self-discipline alone became the test of commitment to Communist principles. Spartan self-denial in identifying with and working among the masses replaced concepts of élitist leadership by a somewhat remote government.

Mao's tough new policy was applied rigorously to all Party members. There were no promises of reward other than the spiritual satisfaction of contributing to ultimate victory. Even those in the highest leadership circles in Yenan lived a simple, frugal life, with their

Statue and mausoleum of Dr. Norman Bethune, located in a park commemorating revolutionary heroes in Shih-chia-chuang.

clothing, food, and accommodation in sharp contrast to the relative luxury affected by Kuomintang civil and military leaders. In Communist areas, training schools instilled these attitudes in new recruits. These teachings were reinforced, in 1942– 4, by a Rectification Campaign, which was essentially a series of forums for all Party members. In small groups or mass meetings, members were subjected to intense public criticism and self-examination, designed to heighten and perfect the revolutionary spirit.

The Yenan years bore fruit in the civil war with the Kuomintang after 1945. The Nationalist forces were substantially larger than the

Communist. Moreover, they were better equipped, possessing heavy artillery, aircraft, naval units, tanks, and other sophisticated materials of a modern military force, while Communist equipment was often homemade, captured from the Japanese, or later, taken from dead or captured Kuomintang soldiers. The Kuomintang held south and central China, which included the richest agricultural area and the major centres of industry and commerce. Furthermore, the Nationalists could count on continued, if increasingly reluctant, American support.

But Communist strength lay precisely where the Kuomintang was weak. Years of experience had evolved a more flexible military strategy, based on guerilla warfare, whenever direct confrontation threatened serious losses. The Communists put their faith more in men than in military hardware. They possessed a dedicated core of Party members and soldiers who believed in their cause, who had been hardened by long years of warfare and discipline, and who had a relaxed confidence in moving and working among the common people. They revered their revolutionary martyrs and heroes, including a Canadian, Dr. Norman Bethune, who had died in 1939 after serving only slightly more than a year as a medical officer with the Communist partisan forces. The CCP began the civil war with relatively small numbers and inferior equipment. In the end, their numbers were swollen by Kuomintang defectors and waves of new recruits, and their forces became increasingly better armed as Nationalist troops, in hasty retreat, abandoned their new American equipment and munitions. The Communist victory in 1949 was evidence of the critical importance of human factors in overcoming a technically superior but unmotivated enemy.

Analysis

1. What conclusions would Marx have come to regarding the stage of development reached by China in the 1920s? Would he consider the country ready for revolution? Why?

2. "To sum up, the Long March ended with our victory and the enemy's defeat." To what extent was Mao's evaluation of the Long March an accurate one?

3. Compare the strategy used by the CCP during the Japanese occupation with that used by the Kuomintang. Explain why the two strategies differed so widely.

4. Explain why Mao made changes in Marxist–Leninist philosophy and strategy.

Suggested Readings

J. Ch'en, *Mao and the Chinese Revolution* (London: Oxford University Press, 1965).
    An excellent tracing of Mao's early life and thought, up to the triumph of 1949.

Hsüeh Chün-tu, ed., *Revolutionary Leaders of Modern China* (London: Oxford University Press, 1971).
    Section III, ''The Communist Movement,'' contains a number of good studies of various Communist figures in the early movement.

Edgar Snow, *Red Star Over China* (New York: Grove Press, 1938).
    By far the best contemporary description of the Yenan period, this book, by an American reporter fluent in Chinese, has deservedly become a classic.

Roderick Stewart, *Bethune* (Don Mills: Paperjacks, 1975).
    A recent study of the life of Canada's chief participant in the Chinese Communist revolution.

Dick Wilson, *The Long March, 1935: The Epic of Chinese Communism's Survival* (London: Hamish Hamilton, 1971).
    The best concentrated study of the history and effect of this key event in CCP history.

CHAPTER 14
The Grand Experiment

Chronology

1949 People's Political Consultative Conference passes Organic Law (September); declaration of People's Republic of China (October 1).
1950–3 Korean War; Marriage Law proclaimed.
1954 Constitution replaces Organic Law of 1949.

In September 1949, on the eve of proclaiming the People's Republic of China (PRC), Mao Tse-tung declared: "Our nation will never again be an insulted nation. We have stood up."[46] This announcement signified both an end and a beginning: national weakness and humiliation belonged to the past; to the future belonged the on-going revolution. The consolidation of political power under the Communists, Mao insisted, was only the first step in the transformation of China into a new society, as defined by Marxism–Leninism. Revolution had to be a continuing process, and revolutionary fervour was essential as a motive force for further change. Mao's words and thoughts go a long way toward explaining the course of Chinese history since 1949.

New Political Frameworks

In 1949, the Communist regime declared the inauguration of New Democracy. In substance, this was the moderate political program outlined in 1940 by Mao Tse-tung during the Yenan exile. Its purpose was to recruit support from all non-hostile political groups, while maintaining the democratic centralist principles of Lenin:

China can now adopt a system of people's congresses—the people's national congress, the people's provincial congresses, the people's country congresses, the people's district congresses, down to the people's township congresses—and let these congresses at various levels elect the organs of government. But a system of really universal and equal suffrage, irrespective of sex, creed, property, or education, must be put into practice so that the organs of government elected can properly represent each revolutionary class according to its status in the state, express the people's will and direct revolutionary struggles, and embody the spirit of New Democracy. Such a system is democratic centralism.[47]

In September 1949, a People's Political Consultative Conference passed a provisional constitutional framework for the New Democracy. Dominated by the CCP, though also attended by representatives of forty-five other political parties and groups, the Conference elaborated on the practice of democratic centralism:

The organs of state power at all levels shall practice democratic centralism. In doing this the main principles shall be: the People's Congresses shall be responsible and accountable to the people; the People's Government Councils shall be responsible and accountable to the People's Congresses. Within the People's Congresses and within the People's Government Councils, the minority shall abide by the decisions of the majority; the appointment of the People's Government of each level shall be ratified by the People's Government of the higher level; the People's Governments of the lower levels shall obey the People's Governments of the higher levels and all local People's Governments throughout the country shall obey the Central People's Government.[48]

The New Democracy, then, demanded minority subordination to the majority, and the obedience of individuals and lower-level governments to the higher central authorities.

In answer to possible objections that this new system was more dictatorial than democratic, Mao replied on July 1, 1949:

"You are dictatorial." Dear sirs, you are right; that is exactly what we are. The experience of several decades, amassed by the Chinese people, tells us to carry out the people's democratic dictatorship. That is, the right of reactionaries to voice their opinions must be abolished and only the people are allowed to have the right of voicing their opinions.

Who are the "people"? At the present stage in China, they are the working class, the peasant class, the petty bourgeoisie, and national bourgeoisie. Under the leadership of the working class and the CP [Communist Party], these classes unite together to form their own state and elect their own government (so as to) carry out a dictatorship over the lackeys of imperialism—the landlord class, the bureaucratic capitalist class, and the KMT reactionaries and their henchmen representing these classes—to suppress them, allowing them only to behave properly and not to talk and act wildly. If they talk and act wildly their (action) will be prohibited and punished immediately. The democratic system is to be carried out within the ranks of the people, giving them freedom of speech, assembly, and association. The right to vote is given only to the people and not to the reactionaries. These two aspects, namely, democracy among the people and dictatorship over the reactionaries, combine to form the people's democratic dictatorship.[49]

Attitude and action were fundamental; "reactionaries" could, in time, rejoin the ranks of the "people," after undergoing a change of heart and after a demonstration of socialist convictions.

Two formal political power structures—state organizations and party organizations—embodied these ideas after 1949 (see structural chart, page 180). However, to complete the picture of political power (as distinct from structure), we must add a third element—the People's Liberation Army, which played an important civil role. This triad interrelated at all levels, as the relationships of state, party, and army were close and their functions overlapping. The Chinese Communist system did not attempt the clear-cut division of powers or functions common to western political structures.

On paper, at least, the Organic Law (1949) of the New Democracy and the Constitution which replaced it (1954) created an elaborate state structure for the new China. A system of People's Congresses, elected by universal suffrage, extended from the village level to the National People's Congress. Appended to this hierarchy of congresses was a network of formal administrative units. At the top was the Standing Committee of the National People's Congress. Real day-to-day administrative responsibility, however, lay with the next level, the pow-

Structural Chart
(simplified)

State Organizations
(1954 Constitution)

Party Organizations
(according to 1956 Constitution)

National People's Congress
1954 —
1 226 delegates

Chairman of the People's Republic
(1949–58 — Mao Tse-tung)
(1959–68 — Liu Shao-ch'i)
(1968–75 — vacant, or Acting Chairman)
(1975 — post eliminated)

Chairman of the Central Committee
1949–76 —
Mao Tse-tung

National Party Congress

Standing Committee

State Council

Premier
1949–76 —
Chou En-lai

Central Committee

Political Bureau (Politburo)

Standing Committee

Ministries & Commissions

Provincial & Lower Level Administrative Units

Central Control Commission

Secretariat

Departments of Central Committee

Provincial People's Congresses

Municipal, County, Prefectural, & Township Level Congresses

Lower Level Party Organizations

Provincial & Lower Level Party Units

- - - - - - - -> elects (according to Constitutions)

————————> practical (de facto) controls

=============> responsible to

Adapted from: D. J. Waller, *The Government and Politics of Communist China* (London: Hutchinson, 1970), 51, 98.

erful State Council, which consisted of the Premier, Vice-Premiers, and Ministers of the various departments, commissions, and agencies of the central bureaucracy.

These formal organizations of congresses and accompanying bureaucratic administrative units played important roles, although at first glance they may seem extremely limited. Congresses were only minimally legislative in purpose. At various levels within the country, their prime function was to provide: (a) local reactions to central policy directives; and (b) some feeling of popular participation in the governmental process as a whole. Article 2 of the 1954 Constitution read:

> All power in the People's Republic of China belongs to the people. The organs through which the people exercise power are the National People's Congress and the local people's congresses.
>
> The National People's Congress, the local people's congresses and other organs of state without exception practise democratic centralism.[50]

How these congresses worked in practice is explained by a modern scholar:

> In accordance with this law [of March 1, 1953, governing the election of deputies to the People's Congresses], qualified citizens in the basic-level units (i.e., administrative *hsiang* or villages, towns, and wards within cities) held elections in 1953 and early 1954 for deputies to the basic-level people's congresses. These congresses soon elected deputies to the county, and city people's congresses, and in June and July 1954 the county and city people's congresses met. Among other things, they elected deputies to the provincial people's congresses. In the following month, the provincial people's congresses and the People's Liberation Army elected deputies to the National People's Congress.
>
> . . .
>
> . . . Insofar as enlisting popular support was concerned, the holding of general elections, particularly those on the grass-roots level in which hundreds of millions of people took part, and the election of millions of deputies to the people's congresses at various levels apparently imbued many of the participants with a sense of involvement in the affairs of the state, despite the omnipresence of the CCP's strong guiding hand. At least some of those who were elected as deputies were apt to be susceptible to such additional influences as the prestige and material perquisites accruing

to their status. Since the deputies were leaders or model workers in various fields, their closer identification with the regime could only strengthen the latter's hold on the nation, and periodical elections and convening of the people's congresses make it possible for the CCP to derive this benefit continuously. That political activists indeed prize membership in the people's congresses can be seen from the fact that in 1963 the regime decided to expand the congresses at all levels. The Third National People's Congress elected in 1964, for example, was more than twice as large as its two predecessors elected in 1954 and 1959.[51]

As in all other countries, the "civil service" administrative units, alongside every level of the congresses, handled all the bureaucratic tasks of running a modern society. At the centre, as the director of the country's formal state structure, stood Chou En-lai, Premier from 1949 until his death in early 1976. Always an important figure among the leaders, he never played an analogous role to that of an American president or a prime minister in the British parliamentary tradition. His primary function was the skilful direction of the state bureaucratic structure.

The Communist Party paralleled the official governmental bodies. According to the Party Constitution, the National Party Congress was the Party's ultimate governing body, representing all levels of Party membership in the same way (i.e., deputies at one level selecting the representatives of the next higher level) as the National People's Congress. Similarly, the very size of the National Party Congress limited its activities. Between 1921 and 1969, there were only nine such National Party Congresses (the Seventh in 1945, the Eighth in 1956, and the Ninth in 1969). The Party's Central Committee, elected by the Party Congress to exercise general supervisory authority between its meetings, had nearly two hundred members:

> The Central Committee is an assemblage of all the important Chinese Communist leaders, who, holding multiple strategic positions in the party, the government, the armed forces, and the people's organizations, have effective control over all aspects of national life. Thus, the importance of the Central Committee lies not so much in what it formally does at its plenums as in the authority that its members individually wield in their fields of operation and the influence committeemen can exert on the

Politburo by virtue of their relatively easy access to members of that more exclusive club.[52]

The Politburo (a short form for Political Bureau), and especially its inner working group, the Standing Committee, was the centre of policy formulation and decision-making. Members usually held concurrent high posts in the central state structure, and the Standing Committee was made up of the country's most powerful leaders. It consisted of the Chairman of the Central Committee (Mao Tse-tung) and six to eight other high-ranking leaders such as Premier Chou En-lai.

Policy decisions flowed from the Standing Committee, through the Politburo, to a Secretariat. The latter steered them through various subcommittees of the Central Committee and then passed these directives down through the Party units at every level in the country. The Central Control Commission and similar control commissions at all other levels of the Party were the chief overseers of Party members' discipline.

While Party membership (which was highly prized) included only two to three per cent of the population and rarely constituted a majority in local governmental bodies, the Party members were the active core of such bodies, particularly in directing discussions on the means of implementing central policy guidelines and adapting them to local conditions. Party committees have been called the "alter ego" of the formal state structure; they could be found everywhere, in government bureaus, factories, schools, communes, or military companies. It was the Party's constant and active presence that was one key to China's political unity after 1949.

The People's Liberation Army (PLA) formed the third portion of the organizational structure of post-1949 China. In the early 1950s the large forces which had won the last battles of the civil war were partially demobilized and replaced with highly professional, smaller armed forces. At that time, the PLA was assigned a primarily military role, with few civil functions except in border regions or in large-scale public works projects. This changed in the late 1950s, and, as part of the shift, Lin Piao (1907–71), who became Minister of Defence in

1959, rose steadily to political prominence within the central leadership. As in the Yenan years, the PLA became an important partner in state and party activities, acting, whenever called upon, as a reserve labour corps, a governmental unit, a social welfare agency, or an inspirational model of proper socialist behaviour. Increasingly, individual PLA members occupied what would normally be considered civil posts within either state or party bureaucracies. Many years before, Mao Tse-tung had laid down the dictum: "The Party commands the gun; the gun will never command the Party." In a structural sense, this meant that the PLA after 1949 was controlled by the Ministry of Defence (a state organization) which in turn was supervised by the Military Affairs Commission of the Party's Central Committee. In a non-structural, operational sense, it meant that, besides being a formidable military establishment, the People's Liberation Army was an active participant in the political life of the nation.

We should not leave this analysis without noting the Chinese attitude toward this elaborate framework. Formal structures and procedures never became viewed as the only way to get things done. The Party Constitution stipulated yearly meetings of the National Party Congress, but the infrequency of those sessions did not really cause any concern to the Chinese. Laws, including the constitutions of party or nation, were declarations of principles and not immutable definitions of structures or procedures. Men and programs, rather than institutional frameworks or formal legislation, were the focus of political life and debate.

An important key to the success of the system lay with individuals known as "cadres." Cadres were not necessarily Party members, nor were all Party members necessarily cadres. The term denoted anyone who held a position of formal responsibility in any organization—the Party, the state, the army, a local neighbourhood association, a factory, or a school. As the leaders within these units of society, they acted as local authorities for the policies of the Party and the state.

Cadres were, however, more than simply transmitters of directives from on high. They were responsible local people who handled daily routine administration and helped to adapt general policy guidelines from higher authorities to the actualities of the local situation. They also served as the vital communication link between the everyday life of the people and the central authorities. The Communist ideal was centralized government and Party authority, complemented by local initiative and popular mass involvement in the revolutionary process. The cadres were the vital link between the two spheres. Part of the revolutionary ideal was a proper balance between the centre and the localities, between uniformity and flexibility, between high-level planning and local initiatives. In practice, maintaining this balance proved very difficult, and the difficulties encountered, as well as the varying degrees of success with which these were solved, are more important for understanding post-1949 China than any studies of the formal modifications of the legislative structure.

The Mass Line

The relationship between the masses on the one hand and the leaders, cadres, and Party members on the other, was a matter of central concern in Mao's thinking on the new China. The model for this relationship was set out by Mao in 1943:

> We Communists must be able to integrate ourselves with the masses in all things. If our Party members spend their whole lives sitting indoors and never go out to face the world and brave the storm, what good will they be to the Chinese people? . . . We should go to the masses and learn from them, synthesize their experience into better, articulated principles and methods, then do propaganda among the masses, and call upon them to put these principles and methods into practice so as to solve their problems and help them achieve liberation and happiness.[53]

Cadres adhering to this Mass Line had to combine living and working among the common people with diligent study of Marxist–Leninist theory, as interpreted by Mao Tse-tung. It was a call for a life of selfless service, and the chief reward was the work itself. It required that cadres lead rather than command, that they learn as well as educate, and that they stimulate the masses rather than make decisions for them. The people themselves were to carry out the revolution. These high ideals, though not always upheld after 1949, remained an unbroken thread in Chinese Communist history.

The same tough standards were set down for the country's armed forces. "Serve the People" became the slogan of the People's Liberation Army. Thoroughly indoctrinated in the Mass Line, PLA members inherited the legacy of the Red Army of Yenan days. Its public heroes always epitomized selfless social service as well as military exploits, and the roots of their heroism always lay in political principles rather than simply individual courage. Army membership was honoured within Chinese society, much sought after by the young, and difficult to obtain. Increasingly reinforced after 1957 by the swelling millions of a People's Militia, the armed strength of China did not suffer by the participation of its professional forces in social, political, and economic activities in addition to performing their military responsibilities.

The ideal of a revolution carried out by the people meant a constant

Gate of Heavenly Peace (T'ien-an men), leading into Forbidden City. The huge square in front of the gate was built after 1949 for mass parades and demonstrations.

effort toward the political involvement of the masses. Block or ward associations in cities, and peasant associations in rural regions, sprang up in large numbers immediately upon Liberation. Labour unions, women's associations, and other special-interest groups were quickly organized. Stimulated by local Party members, such groups engaged in adult-literacy campaigns, hygiene and health programs, and the organization of local welfare services. Officially recognized and financially supported by the government, they represented another channel linking all citizens with the central system. Supplementing state, party, or army structures, these mass organizations brought various campaigns for greater production or purer revolutionary values down to the level of every Chinese. No member of the society had the right to remain uninvolved, and all became participants in some kind of organized activity.

Foreign Policy

While the main concern of the war-weary Chinese Communists after 1949 was the internal revolution, foreign affairs could not be set aside. Almost immediately, they found themselves involved in a conflict in Korea. Korea was part of the Japanese Empire from 1910 until 1945, when it was divided by the Russians and the Americans, the former occupying the north as far as the 38th Parallel, and the latter the south. As the wartime alliance between Russia and the West broke down in the postwar years, each of the two occupying powers sponsored a separate Korean native government. The Russians withdrew their troops from North Korea in December 1948, and the Americans withdrew from South Korea in June 1949. War between the two sections of the country broke out in June 1950.

"Who attacked whom?" remains a continuing debate.[54] At the time, the western countries insisted that North Korea was the aggressor. From a western perspective, the Korean War was a test of new postwar collective security arrangements. During a brief period when Russia boycotted the United Nations Security Council, the U.N. branded North Korea as the aggressor and offered military aid to the

South Korean government. After 1949, Peking had publicly declared a foreign policy of "leaning to one side," which meant emphasizing relations with Russia and other members of the socialist or communist bloc. Communist China, and indeed the entire bloc, insisted that the invasion had been initiated by South Korea. The Chinese viewed U.N. intervention in this neighbouring country as simply an extension of a hostile anti-communist American foreign policy, particularly since the U.N. contingent in South Korea was predominantly American and the Supreme Commander of U.N. troops, General Douglas MacArthur, was also an American.

The U.N. forces, in the fall of 1950, pushed north of the 38th Parallel and overran most of North Korea. China's concern deepened. The U.N. Supreme Command also refused to guarantee respect for the Manchurian boundary between Chinese and Korean territory, and U.N. planes bombed bridges across the Yalu River border line. In response, China moved into Korea with "volunteers" and gave massive aid to the North Korean forces, driving back the U.N. advance. After a long stalemate and two years of negotiations, an armistice ended the war in July 1953, with Korea again divided roughly along the 38th Parallel.

The Chinese continued to be apprehensive about western, and particularly American, intentions. The U.S., in turn, was caught in a rising domestic scare about the "communist menace" and remained suspicious of Chinese ambitions. Diplomatic relations between Peking and Washington had ceased shortly after the establishment of the People's Republic of China. As part of a "containment" policy, the U.S. planned a series of military outposts in an attempt to draw a semicircle around China. The U.S. also pressed for an international commercial and diplomatic boycott of Red China. After a brief hesitation, once the Korean War broke out, Washington renewed its support for the Kuomintang regime in Taiwan, or Nationalist China. For two decades the Americans led the battle against U.N. recognition of the PRC, insisting that the Nationalist regime was the legitimate and sole representative of all Chinese.

Other western countries never fully subscribed to the American view. As early as January 1950, Britain recognized the PRC, but the British initiative did not meet with Chinese enthusiasm. Not until mid-1954 (after the Korean Armistice) were formal diplomatic relations re-established, and then only on the intermediate level of missions under chargés d'affaires, and not by an exchange of ambassadors. Other western countries, including Finland, Denmark, Sweden, Holland, and Switzerland, did recognize the PRC and they established formal relations in 1950; these countries were joined by Spain in 1952.

Trade with the West was slow to grow, partly as a result of China's own wishes to trade primarily within the "socialist bloc." An American-inspired trade embargo, agreed to by other western powers during the Korean War, was relaxed in the mid-1950s because of pressure by Britain and other countries. Soon after emerging from its postwar American occupation, Japan began to trade with China, and the volume grew steadily, despite continued strained governmental relations between the two countries.

Canadian trade remained negligible until the late 1950s. The Canadian embassy in China was closed in early 1950, but no ambassador was named to Taiwan. Ottawa's tentative moves toward a possible resumption of relations halted with the outbreak of the Korean War, when support from the United Nations brought Canadian troops into the Korean conflict. It was a full decade after the end of that war before the first hesitant steps were taken, in the mid-1960s, toward Canada's gradual disassociation from the anti-recognition bloc within the U.N.

The Early Revolutionary Program

Despite recurrent problems in foreign affairs, the main thrust of Chinese energy after 1949 remained directed toward internal social and economic change. The spirit of the new social revolution is well illustrated in the Marriage Law of 1950. This legislation broke the traditional hold of family and clan over the lives of their young men and women. Marriage and divorce were now unequivocally made the sole concern of the individuals involved, rather than being matters for family decision. Women were further freed from their traditional subordination to male authority, as the law made male and female equal partners in the marriage itself. Not content with leaving these changes as legal blueprints, the Communists made them matters for public discussion through the various mass organizations that reached into every part of the country.

Clashing interpretations (both Chinese and foreign) of the Marriage Law reflect the problems of assessing objectively a revolution as fundamental and swift-moving as that of post-1949 China. Many outsiders considered the legislation as destructive of the warmth and security offered by the traditional Chinese family structure, and they condemned it as being motivated by a Communist desire to extend state control. Others hailed it as a sterling example of Communist commitment to idealistic reform, pointing out that it brought liberation from a repressive social tradition to millions of people. Whichever viewpoint outsiders might take, the results of the Marriage Law for the Communists were both ideologically satisfying and politically useful. Such new social practices marked a fundamental break with the practices of the past, and the chief benefactors—in this case, youth, and especially women—responded with support for the new order.

Only increased agricultural production could feed China's growing population and provide the necessary capital for rapid industrial advance. To accomplish these goals, the new regime concentrated more on changes in rural social relations than on investment of scarce capital and equipment in large-scale projects. The Communists blamed the country's chronic economic problems primarily on the rural class system with its rigid social hierarchy and its exploitation of the peasant. Immediately after proclaiming the People's Republic, the new regime launched a national land reform campaign with the goal of eliminating the traditional system. The Communists sponsored local mass meetings to decide issues of confiscation and redistribution of land and other property. At mass public trials, where all those assembled made the decisions, the most hated of the ex-landlords were condemned to execution, while the rest were judged redeemable through "re-education." In the redistribution of property, the richer peasantry fared less well than the great majority classified as "middle" or "poor" peasants. The Communists did not seek absolute egalitarianism; their aim was to eliminate a social class (the landlord-gentry) which lived by the labour of others, and so release the energies of the peasantry for greater agricultural production.

Land reform in the early 1950s created a nation of small peasant landowners, but this represented only the initial step in the regime's ultimate aims. The Communists immediately sought greater efficiency by encouraging mutual-aid teams of five or more households, and eventually, co-operatives of thirty or more families became common. Pooled labour worked the land, which remained privately owned, and income was distributed according to contributions of land and labour. Government quotas set production targets, incentives were offered for consolidating fragmented and uneconomical holdings, and set prices were paid by the government for surplus products.

By 1956, when such co-operatives included about sixty per cent of the rural populace, the regime moved into the new stage of consolidation. Again using a massive propaganda campaign, the Communists urged the merging of the co-operatives into larger collective farms, based on entire villages. Land and tools were now owned collectively, and only small vegetable plots were retained under private cultivation. The peasants derived their major income from participation in a common farming program. By the summer of 1958, some 750 000 collective farms had been organized throughout the country.

Marx had envisaged an industrial base as a condition for a modern socialist society moving toward communism. Although Mao had, at the outset, decided to build the Chinese revolution upon the peasant, the Communists did not deny the importance of industrial development. By the end of 1956 most private factories had become "joint enterprises." Nevertheless, private owners who had not fled abroad or been condemned as enemies of the state received a guaranteed return of interest on their capital investments, while the state took over the total direction of production as well as the setting of wages and benefits for the workers. The state also assumed control of foreign trade, and domestic private trade dwindled to only small-scale retail

Rapid development of industrial strength has been a major objective of post-1949 Chinese policy, as demonstrated by this massive open-pit coal mine in northeastern China.

enterprises. Following the Russian model, a series of Five-Year Plans was instituted to spur industrial development, particularly in heavy industry.

Right from the beginning, and increasingly as time went on, Communist industrial planning deliberately favoured new areas, particularly in the interior, over the already-industrialized urban centres of the coastal regions. This policy served many purposes. It spread the industrial base, and so reduced military vulnerability (initially, the Chinese feared American hostility; in later years they were more concerned about Russia). It brought manufacturing closer to natural resources and domestic markets, thereby saving on transportation costs. It also curbed the influence and growth of Shanghai and other "bourgeois" centres. Economists might argue that this dispersal of scarce capital and expertise was inefficient. On the other hand, widely spread industrial development benefited a broader portion of the people.

All these measures aroused very divergent responses in outside observers. Some condemned land reform for its attack on private property and accused the new regime of carrying out a massive blood-

Workshop in Shanghai Diesel Engine Plant, producing engines for China's new shipbuilding industry.

bath. These critics similarly viewed collectivization as a cruel trick, forced upon a peasantry taken in by the recent redistribution that had bestowed privately owned plots of land upon individuals. Commentators more sympathetic to the regime defended land reform. They pointed out that the mass trials, though conducted by Party members, nevertheless did involve the peasantry in the making of the new society, and furthermore, for the first time in history, provided justice (if rough justice) for their legitimate grievances. They also noted that far more ex-landlords were considered redeemable than were executed. Some writers accepted the Communists' claim that collectivization sprang from the demands of the peasants themselves; others pointed out that the transformation of agriculture was brought about by central policy decision and the skilful use of propaganda, with persuasion and popular discussion minimizing the need for open coercion.

However we weigh these outside opinions, in the eyes of the Communists the path toward socialism demanded an end of exploitation in "feudal" relationships (referring to landlords) and "capitalist" relationships (referring to bureaucrats, businessmen, and industrialists). To the Communists, the disappearance of small-scale, private landownership was a proper sequel to the elimination of owner-ship by landlords. Economically, collectivization was justified on the grounds of its potential for greater agricultural production, which provided a higher living standard for the rural population, as well as a surplus to support the industrial program. As for methods of im-plementation, the Communists used waves of propaganda and or-ganized discussion sessions to ensure that resistance would be over-come by collective pressure rather than by a naked use of state power. One of the aims of the revolution—rapid progress toward a socialist society—was achieved, while the Mass Line philosophy, that the revolution must not only benefit the masses but also be carried out by them, had at least the appearance of having been followed.

Analysis

1. Compare the political structure of China and that of your country. Analyse the extent to which each appears to be democratic and the extent to which each is democratic in practice.

2. Chinese foreign policy since 1949 has been variously described as "aggressive" by some and as "remarkably restrained" by others. How would you describe it? Select examples to support your view.

3. The CCP policy on land reform was the most fundamentally revolutionary act in bringing about the new society. Discuss.

4. Do you agree with the cities or the supporters of the new regime's early policies? Explain.

Suggested Readings

Jerome Ch'en, ed., *Mao* (Englewood Cliffs, N.J.: Prentice-Hall, 1969).
  Excellent selection of extracts from Mao's writings through the years, supplemented by several short essays on various aspects of his contribution to communist theory and practice.
William Hinton, *Fan-shen: A Documentary of Revolution in a Chinese Village* (New York: Vintage Books, 1966).
  A graphic depiction of land reform and other changes in a north-China village in the initial period of Communist power.
Stuart R. Schram, *Mao Tse-tung* (New York: Simon & Schuster, 1966).
  A biography of Chairman Mao with an accompanying history of the Chinese Communist Party.

CHAPTER 15
The Great Leap

Chronology
1956–7 Hundred Flowers Campaign
1957–9 Three Flags Program

By the late 1950s steady progress in both industry and agriculture was evident, but its slowness frustrated impatient revolutionaries. The size of the population posed major problems: feeding some 500 million people in 1949 was a formidable task, but by the late 1950s the numbers had swelled to an estimated 650 million. Traditional social attitudes concerning the desirability of large families were reinforced by Marxist economic theory, which blamed poverty on socio-economic relationships which put curbs on production, rather than on over-population. (Birth control was available through state auspices from the 1950s, but was not encouraged by a sustained mass campaign until the mid-1960s). Under the pressure of rising numbers, it was difficult to build up a surplus of capital to support rapid industrialization. As Marxist–Leninist–Maoists, the Chinese Communists sought greater productivity in stepped-up socialization and increased revolutionary motivation. The result was the Three Flags Program, consisting of the establishment of communes, the Great Leap, and the Socialist Construction Movement. The program was commonly given the single label, the Great Leap.

Launched in 1957, this program sought a radical breakthrough in agricultural productivity and industrial development. In rural areas the commune now replaced co-operatives and collective farms. Although the 26 000 communes did vary greatly in size and population, their basic pattern was similar. Every twenty or so households formed a "production team," and each eight to ten production teams formed a "production brigade," usually corresponding to the old village community. Twenty to forty such brigades constituted a commune, which might include as many as 50 000 people (the average was 25 000) and extend over several thousand hectares. Attempts to further "proletarianize" rural China included the experimental elimination of all private vegetable plots and the organization of communal mess halls.

As part of the Great Leap, industrial production was everywhere encouraged. Backyard blast furnaces and small manufacturing shops sprouted throughout the country. Communes tried to add processing and even manufacturing to their agricultural activities. In urban areas, factory or residential-area projects relied on the extra labour of people when they had completed their normal tasks. Campaign slogans urged everyone's involvement during their off-hours. By such means the Communists hoped that China could greatly accelerate economic development and, within a few decades, surpass Britain (their chosen example of western industrial strength) in basic industrial production.

Socialist Construction, the last part of the Three Flags Program, meant a greater commitment to the ideals of socialism as the means of accomplishing these economic goals. An attempt was made, both in rural communes and in urban centres, to relate income more to need than to acquired skills, seniority, or even productivity; psychological rewards were to replace material incentives. The regime also tried to de-emphasize technological expertise in favour of socialist motivation, hoping to achieve industrialization as much by enthusiasm and politics as by capital accumulation and formal technical training. For example, the idealistic proponents of the program felt that a group of peasants could sit down together, with clear and simple instructions, and construct a workable blast furnace out of locally available materials, their devotion and collective effort substituting for their lack of engineering skills. The product might be cruder, but in the eyes of the committed, the economic and social benefits more than compensated for any shortcomings.

Western observers, especially the Russians, looked askance at these planning methods and felt vindicated when the Chinese effort faltered badly. A typical quip characterized the Great Leap as ''a small skip'' if not ''a backward stumble.'' Economic statistics bore out this scepticism. By 1959, to their considerable embarrassment, the Chinese Communists were having to scale down drastically the enthusiastic claims of productive gains made in the previous year. These, it turned out, had been based on local cadres reporting their zealous hopes rather than actual production figures. A series of bad harvests provided a major setback to the program, which was already showing signs that the enthusiasm of the rural populace for such heavy physical demands on their workday was dwindling. To avoid famine, the regime had to purchase large quantities of food abroad. Suddenly Canadian wheat sales to China rose from a trickle to about 1.26 million kilolitres in 1960 and more than doubled the following year. The backyard furnaces that had sprung up everywhere proved wasteful, and their products were mostly useless without costly reprocessing, for which there were no foundries. Political differences between Peking and Moscow suddenly escalated, leading to the abrupt withdrawal, in 1960, of Russian aid teams, who left behind them many unfinished capital projects and stockpiles of unfamiliar machinery. The Chinese lacked the trained personnel, and even the blueprints, to complete these projects.

The euphoria of the Great Leap gave way to sober reassessment. Significant changes in policy were soon evident. Private vegetable plots reappeared in rural areas, and the few experiments under way in fostering urban communes disappeared. Pay-scale differentials and material incentives quietly reappeared everywhere. Significantly, in late 1959 Mao Tse-tung (the most prominent advocate of reliance on ideological commitment) stepped down as Chairman of the People's Republic, a position taken over a few months later by Liu Shao-ch'i, one of the most prominent exponents of more cautious and conventional development policies.

In spite of its shortcomings, to view the Great Leap as an unmitigated disaster may well be a distortion. Much had been learned from this monumental attempt to change society. If the products of the backyard furnaces proved unusable, nevertheless millions of untrained peasants had tried their hand at basic industrial processes. Many of the smaller factories, such as those on the communes that turned out irrigation piping or agricultural tools, did remain in operation. And even though the work team or brigade, rather than the larger commune, now became the basic units of economic planning and shared earnings, the rural commune structure survived as a co-ordinating framework and the primary social-service unit. Any detailed economic analyses of Chinese production after 1958 are educated guesses (the Chinese having since then refrained from releasing full statistical data), but there is sufficient evidence to indicate that the steady rise in Chinese net productivity received only a slight and brief setback at the height of the Great Leap period.

The Nature of the Commune

As communes remain a basic feature of contemporary Chinese social structure, it would be useful to look at one of them in some detail. The example used is the New China Commune just outside Canton; the description is based on the notes of a Canadian professor who visited the commune in 1971.[55] At that time the commune consisted of 13 500 families, or a total of 61 000 people, divided into 326 production teams. Located in the rich soil and moist climate of the river delta surrounding Canton, 85% of the 5 200 hectares under cultivation in the commune was riceland. Besides growing grain and vegetables, the commune had a poultry industry and a fish farm. It also raised pigs, with 60% of pig production in private hands.

The commune leaders claimed that their rice output was three times the pre-1949 figure and twice the amount produced on the same land prior to the commune's foundation in 1958. A fair part of this achievement was attributed to local initiative. For example, a loan obtained from the local county government had enabled commune

Sampans on a commune outside Canton in south China (upper); shopping area of a commune near Nanking in central China (lower).

Small industry producing agricultural tools on a commune near Peking in north China.

members to build three water reservoirs and a complex of irrigation canals to prevent drought damage, as well as some forty kilometres of dams to prevent flooding. Increased production served both the members of the commune and the nation. Of the commune's production, 25% went to the state, 30% to 40% was consumed, and the remainder was available as a reserve within the commune or for sale for capital to invest in further development.

Although agriculture was the chief economic activity, the commune contained some nineteen small factories as well. Mechanization by North American standards was not very far advanced, but by pre-1949 Chinese standards it was much more widespread. Approximately 80% of the peasants' homes were now electrified, whereas twenty years earlier, electrical power had been virtually unknown in rural areas. Electricity was also used for the pumping stations that powered the new irrigation system. The commune owned three trucks and about eighty-five tractors of various sizes, mostly of the garden-tractor variety. Nevertheless, an estimated 60% of the work of the commune was still done by manual labour, oxen, or water-buffalo. Threshing was done by some 1 200 small, portable threshing machines, operated by foot-powered pedals, all produced in one of the commune's own factories. In addition, the commune operated its own coal mine, primarily to provide raw material for its nitrogen factory which made inorganic fertilizer for its own fields; excess produce was sold to neighbouring communes.

The New China Commune was a social unit as well as an economic organization. Each brigade had a primary school, while the commune supported one central high school. Correspondingly, each brigade had its own small medical centre, supplemented by the commune's central hospital of twenty beds, staffed by five nurses, eight doctors, and two dentists. Medical personnel within the commune numbered over one hundred in all, ranging from surgeons to people who had only practical skills and were known as barefoot doctors. Like rural electrification, such medical service in the countryside represented a major advance—before 1949, health care and medical treatment was simply beyond the economic means of most peasants.

This picture of Chinese life, and others like it, have been challenged as being much too rosy. Sceptics have disputed the accuracy of statistics given to western visitors. They have claimed that visitors are duped by the Chinese Communists who let them see only "model" communes, created for propaganda purposes. Actually, the numbers and geographic spread of the communes visited by western observers in recent years provide a great deal of evidence against such views. The reports of visitors, whatever their personal political beliefs, agree that a fundamental transformation in the health and material well-being of the average Chinese peasant has occurred since 1949.

Education and Culture

Debate still rages over the question of spiritual and cultural progress in the People's Republic. A Marxist view of cultural change, but reflecting the particular Chinese situation, was expressed by Mao Tse-tung as far back as 1940:

> A given culture is the ideological reflection of the politics and economics of a given society. There is in China an imperialist culture which is a

reflection of imperialist rule, or partial rule, in the political and economic fields. This culture is fostered not only by the cultural organizations run directly by the imperialists in China but by a number of Chinese who have lost all sense of shame. Into this category falls all culture which reflects her semi-feudal politics and economy, and whose exponents include all those who advocate the worship of Confucius, the study of the Confucian canon, the old ethical code and the old ideas in opposition to the new culture and new ideas. Imperialist culture and semi-feudal culture are devoted brothers and have formed a reactionary cultural alliance against China's new culture. This kind of reactionary cultural alliance served the imperialists and the feudal class and must be swept away.[56]

Thus, according to Mao's analysis, cultural norms, aesthetic perspectives, and literature all had to be involved in the revolutionary process.

Mao was cautious to point out, however, that though the evolution of the new socialist culture could come only through "life-and-death struggle" with the old culture, not everything from the past or from the West should be automatically discarded:

To nourish her own culture, China needs to assimilate a good deal of foreign progressive culture, not enough of which was done in the past. We should assimilate whatever is useful to us today not only from the present-day socialist and new-democratic cultures but also from the earlier cultures of other nations, for example, from the culture of the various capitalist countries in the Age of Enlightenment. However, we should not gulp any of this foreign material down uncritically, but must treat it as we do our food—first chewing it, then submitting it to the working of the stomach and intestines with their juices and secretions, and separating it into nutrient to be absorbed and waste matter to be discarded—before it can nourish us. To advocate "wholesale westernization" is wrong. China has suffered a great deal from the mechanical absorption of foreign material. Similarly, in applying Marxism to China, Chinese communists must fully and properly integrate the universal truth of Marxism with the concrete practice of the Chinese revolution, or in other words, the universal truth of Marxism must be combined with specific national characteristics and acquire a definite national form if it is to be useful, and in no circumstances can it be applied subjectively as a mere formula. Marxists who make a fetish of formulas are simply playing the fool with Marxism and the Chinese revolution, and there is no room for them in the ranks of the Chinese revolution. Chinese culture should have its own form, its own national form. . . .

. . . A splendid old culture was created during the long period of Chinese feudal society. To study the development of this old culture, to reject its feudal dross and assimilate its democratic essence is a necessary condition for developing our new national culture and increasing our national self-confidence, but we should never swallow anything and everything uncritically. It is imperative to separate the fine old culture of the people which had a more or less democratic and revolutionary character from all the decadence of the old feudal ruling class. China's present new politics and new economy have developed out of her old politics and old economy, and her present new culture, too, has developed out of her old culture; therefore, we must respect our own history and must not lop it off. However, respect for history means giving it its proper place as a science, respecting its dialectical development, and not eulogizing the past at the expense of the present or praising every drop of feudal poison.[57]

This critical but not unsympathetic approach to the past and to the West was later summarized in the slogan: "Use the Past to serve the Present; Use the West to serve China."

After 1949, in building the new socialist society, the Communists regarded cultural development as being as important as political and economic reorganization. To guarantee the growth and dissemination of approved cultural attitudes, they employed censorship and control of communications at all levels. "Propaganda" or "indoctrination" did not carry unfavourable connotations; when they were dedicated to ideological goals and the development of the new "socialist man," they were viewed as synonyms for "education."

Education at all levels represented a substantial investment of scarce capital, but despite the underdeveloped state of the economy the Communists have consistently demonstrated a strong commitment to public education. From the beginning, massive adult-literacy campaigns went hand in hand with a rapid expansion of the formal school system. The Chinese rejected western ideas of "liberal education." In the interest of national needs, and to provide schooling for the greatest possible numbers, they unashamedly limited the curriculum mainly to practical technological subjects and a very narrow range of arts subjects. Quotas governed entry into each separate field of study at the upper levels of the educational structure, and specialization in the university meant a specific pattern of courses without options. The ideal graduate was "Red and Expert," that is, a skilled technocrat with the political awareness to guarantee his or her revolutionary commitment. As with army service or Party membership, educated expertise was expected to live up to the injunction, "Serve the People," and to derive its principal reward from its contribution to the collective good.

It is not surprising that the new regime collided with those Chinese intellectuals who retained traditional expectations of receiving both the prestige and the attendant social privileges of high academic achievement. Mao Tse-tung and other Communist leaders possessed high intellectual capabilities and well deserved the honoured label of "intellectuals" in their own right; but their position of power came from political activism rather than educational credentials. They seriously doubted the ideological reliability of intellectuals who had been educated under the old system. After 1949 the regime did bring the intellectuals into the new system—staffing the revitalized and vastly expanded educational and administrative systems—though not without subjecting them to thorough "re-education." Participation in study groups on Marxist thought, involvement in criticism and self-criticism sessions, and public confessions of feudal or reactionary tendencies were required. Those who resisted or who were thought to be too shallow in their re-education could look forward to attending "thought-reform" centres where, removed from normal distractions, they would be "persuaded" to reform themselves through labour and political study.

By 1956 the regime felt confident enough to relax some of its pressure temporarily, under the slogan, "Let a Hundred Flowers bloom together and a Hundred Schools of Thought contend." Secure in its accomplishments, the Party obviously did not expect the harshness and the volume of the attacks that followed. Thorns, instead of flowers, seemed to sprout. Though generally not anti-socialist, the complaints reflected a deep bitterness over tight Party control and discipline.

By late spring 1957, the Hundred Flowers experiment in tolerance ended with a reassertion of strict discipline and an even more vigorous policy of re-education. Two simultaneous campaigns—one of "rectification" against over-enthusiastic and unreliable cadres, the other an "anti-rightist" move to quash the intellectuals' tide of criticism —merged into a single "downward transfer" (*hsia-fang*) movement to send urban teachers, students, and cadres into the rural areas. There they would regain their identification with the masses through hard work, while also helping agricultural production. In 1962 Mao Tsetung called for a massive Socialist Education Movement, which again stressed the study of Mao's political thought and the need for intellectuals to avoid ivory-tower isolation from the society that supported them.

Outside observers responded to the new regime's cultural activities in one of two general ways. Many characterized its efforts as a massive brainwashing of a whole population. According to this view, the system sought to create automatons—obedient creatures without power to make decisions for themselves. These critics argued that the self-criticism and confessions of intellectuals were motivated by a simple desire for self-preservation rather than from any personal conviction. They portrayed these highly educated Chinese as tragic victims of an authoritarian system that denied anyone the right to be uninvolved or to disagree.

According to the other, more sympathetic view, these criticisms ignored the historical context of the Chinese revolution. It was pointed out that the Chinese intellectuals, since the late nineteenth century, had sought the political and social reforms that the Communists finally instituted—mass education, economic development, and women's liberation, all in an independent and proud China. These accomplishments, the supporters maintained, and not massive brainwashing or coercion, explained the intellectuals' acceptance of the need to undergo further reorientation of their thinking. Such observers pointed to the flow back to China of many eminent scholars and scientists, who had had comfortable positions and respectable reputations in western universities before 1949—a return of intellectuals which more than compensated for the few who fled to Hong Kong to escape re-education. They also argued that intellectuals were no more immune than any other element in Chinese society from the necessity to re-examine their ideas and their role in the community. They noted that the Communists did not eliminate the intellectuals (indeed, their commitment to education resulted in the expansion of this class), nor did they reduce them to unthinking obedience; Communist re-education merely sought to integrate intellectuals into the collective efforts of the whole nation. Intellectuals were expected to abandon their traditional élitism and their self-assumed role as independent critics of society and were urged to seek satisfaction (along with other members of society) as active, productive participants in the continuing process of building the new China.

Analysis

1. Discuss the advantages and disadvantages of the commune as an economic and social unit.

2. Have the Chinese introduced too much social and political indoctrination into their educational system? How much is desirable?

3. To what extent does social and political conditioning take place in our educational system?

4. Account for the different views of one group of critics who argue that the Chinese educational system is "brainwashing" and another group who see it as a realization of the goals of twentieth-century Chinese intellectuals.

Suggested Readings

Jan Myrdal, *Report from a Chinese Village* (New York: Signet Books, 1966).
    The result of a Swedish anthropologist's stay in a northern Chinese village in 1962; this is an eloquent description of the life experiences of various villagers.

Michael Okensburg, ed., *The Chinese Development Model* (New York: Praeger, 1973).
    Varied assessments of Chinese views of socialist development.

CHAPTER 16
The Continuing Transition

Chronology
1962 Socialist Education Movement called for by Mao.
1964 PLA under Lin Piao launches Mao-study campaign: "Little Red Book," or
     Quotations from Chairman Mao Tse-tung, published.
1966–9 Great Proletarian Cultural Revolution.
1969 Ninth Party Congress signals end of Cultural Revolution.
1973 Tenth Party Congress denounces deceased Lin Piao.
1975 Fourth National People's Congress adopts new Constitution.
1976 Deaths of Chou En-lai, Chu Teh, and Mao Tse-tung.

Revolution is a violent reaction to legacies of the past and to prevailing social conditions, and Mao Tse-tung's form of Marxism–Leninism is perhaps the world's most relentless revolutionary doctrine in stressing the on-going nature of the struggle. The modern Chinese Communist thinker, unlike his Confucian scholar-official predecessor, looks for a perfect society in the future rather than in a misty, bygone age. Even so, he or she cannot escape the influence of history, and the past lives on within the process of China's continuing struggle for a modern society. The Cultural Revolution of 1966–9, a movement of concentrated revolutionary fervour unleashed against what Mao and others perceived as obstacles from the past as well as spiritual stagnation in the present, nevertheless included an intense search for archaeological findings, revealing a strong interest in China's most ancient foundations. Chairman Mao is known as an accomplished poet and yet, while concentrating on modern themes, his poetry is frequently written in a style that evolved during the T'ang dynasty. In these and many other ways, as we shall see, the continuing revolution in modern China still consciously involved the past. Our brief outline of Chinese history will be concluded with a look at the continuing interaction of tradition and modernity. A word of caution, however, is in order: the events discussed in this chapter are close to us, and we have neither the full data nor the historical perspective for a completely satisfactory analysis.

The Great Proletarian Cultural Revolution

From the earliest stages, the Chinese Communist movement exhibited strong tendencies toward collective leadership. Only a few figures stand out from the general anonymity shrouding their activities, and even these prominent individuals have never assumed the dictatorial power epitomized by Stalin's position within Soviet Russia. Within the Chinese leadership an individual might rise to new influence, undertake new responsibilities, or slip downward in the hierarchy, while outside observers remained unaware, until subsequent events, or the infrequent listing of Politburo members, revealed the change of status. Thus, only by hindsight was it realized that, following the Great Leap of the late 1950s, Mao Tse-tung's influence in the highest echelons of decision-making was drastically weakened. Although Mao remained Chairman of the Party's Central Committee, apparently Liu Shao-ch'i and other leaders took control of both government and Party, relegating Mao to the role of a kind of semi-retired grandfather figure despite his continued high office and his public image as the movement's unchallenged ideologist. Matters did not remain in this state for very long, for China was soon in the throes of revolution once again.

From the perspective of later years it is possible to identify the origins of the Cultural Revolution in the early 1960s. Mao's growing unease over the waning of revolutionary fervour in the Party and in society as a whole was first observable in his call for a Socialist Education Movement in 1962. Largely ignored by state and Party circles, Mao found a sympathetic supporter in Defence Minister Lin Piao, who had a lifelong record of fighting for the CCP cause. In 1964, with Mao's blessing, he launched a "rectification" campaign within the armed forces. Rectification put renewed emphasis on socialist values (the Mass Line): for example, designations of rank on official uniforms were abandoned; high officers were required to take regular stints as common soldiers in the ranks; and PLA members became even more involved, both formally and informally, in non-military activities. It also meant a revitalization of ideological training and revolutionary commitment. For this purpose, the famous "Little Red Book" of extracts from Mao's philosophical writings was published. These short, pithy quotations, which supposedly summarized the essential principles of Maoism in one thin volume, were to be used for guidance in thinking about all matters and in making the multitude of practical decisions required in everyday life.

By 1966 Mao and his supporters, with the backing of a rejuvenated PLA, had embarked on a major program to revive the revolutionary

Red Guards help bind some of the millions of copies of Quotations from Chairman Mao Tse-tung, *the "Little Red Book".*

spirit of the Communist Party and Chinese society. In their view, Party members and cadres had slipped into élitism; forgetting the Mass Line, they had replaced the old pre-Liberation class structure and class attitudes with a new class structure and new class attitudes which threatened the final goal of a truly classless communist society. Faced with a Party and government structure dominated by Liu Shao-ch'i, Mao called upon the Chinese masses, particularly the youth, to purge the system of these reactionary traits. This general appeal, beyond the limits of Party membership, was consistent with Mao's belief that the leaders must never be divorced from the masses and that the people represented the purest motive power within the revolution, if inspired by strong ideological leadership. This was strikingly different from the Russian and Russian-influenced communist systems in which party conflicts were internally settled, without resorting to popular involvement.

Mao's appeal, veiled in oblique references to poisonous influences threatening the future of the revolution, was enthusiastically received. In response to his call, the youth of China formed Red Guard units in high schools and universities. Red Guards joined with other, less organized, non-Party groups in attacking virtually all local evidence of unrevolutionary behaviour or attitude. Initially, the mass demonstrations, the endless public meetings, and the "Big Character," or wall-poster, campaigns showed little coherence or sense of direction. For the most part they attacked unnamed enemies of socialism in positions of authority. Gradually, however, the general focus of the attack (nudged by further cryptic messages of support from Mao and his allies) narrowed down to Liu Shao-ch'i and his followers.

Liu was a battle-tested veteran of the CCP's long struggle for power and a prime moulder of post-1949 Party affairs. From the Yenan years on, his *How to Be a Good Communist* had been a basic text in the training of new Party aspirants. After 1949, many thought that Liu was the logical successor to Mao as leader, especially when, after the failure of the Great Leap, Liu had risen to become Chairman of the People's Republic. Now, however, he and his followers came under attack as the "bourgeois reactionaries" and "capitalist roaders" (i.e., those walking down the road to restoration of capitalism) denounced in the first stages of this Cultural Revolution. Liu fell from power in late 1966 and disappeared from public view (although he was not formally stripped of his chairmanship and other official posts until the Ninth National People's Congress in 1969). Lin Piao, the director of the PLA's rejuvenation, and apparently the creator of the "Little Red Book" mystique, became Mao's closest comrade-in-arms and potential successor.

The Cultural Revolution puzzled outside observers, including the Russians. Mao's attacks on the Party's structure and its members led some western "China watchers" to speculate upon the possible fragmentation of the Communist Party under the attacks of the Red Guard. Experience in their own societies had taught foreign experts to expect a decline in ideological fervour and purity of doctrine once a revolution was brought face to face with the practical needs of modernizing a society. But it was precisely this decline that drew the wrath of Mao and the Red Guard movement. They perceived decay and élitism everywhere and were determined to root out these evils and restore the idealism of the revolution.

Within the context of this massive upheaval, China's disagreements with Russia took on more serious proportions. The dangerous tendencies within Chinese society were blamed, in part, on the Russian example. In earlier, more friendly days, Chinese Communists had looked upon Russia as the heartland of revolution and as the nation that was most advanced in developing a society based on socialist principles. After a brief period of cordial relations in the early 1950s, growing ideological differences and competing national ambitions had strained relations, and in the early 1960s the "Sino-Soviet split" came into the vocabulary of world political analysis. The honeymoon was over. The Chinese, fired with the heady puritanism of their Cultural Revolution, branded Russia guilty of "social revisionism" (a euphemism for abandoning their commitments to the ultimate communist goal of a classless society).

During the height of the Cultural Revolution, critical self-examination was expected of everyone. If that self-examination was deemed insufficient, Red Guards stood ready to conduct mass criticism sessions. Their attacks on the "four olds"—old ideology, old thought, old habits, old customs—were unrestrained. They reviled school authorities and local government officials, and they heaped public ridicule and humiliation on people they considered guilty of unrevolutionary behaviour. Homes were searched and "excessive luxuries" were confiscated and destroyed. Even women's hair-styling and use of cosmetics came under attack as evidence of bourgeois tendencies. Different street signs appeared, bearing bold, revolutionary names. In the Red Guard "invasion" of Peking (they were invited by Mao and travelled to the capital by subsidized transport), foreign embassy personnel briefly suffered harassment. Liu Shao-ch'i, his wife, and many other high government and Party personnel were subjected, by mobs of unruly teenagers, to long, humiliating public harangues against their "crimes." Schools were closed down so that China's youth, who had grown up after 1949, could engage in revolutionary activity and become part of the tradition that had moulded the spirit of the survivors of the Yenan years.

The political upheaval went far beyond the Red Guards' activities. Everywhere, Revolutionary Committees sprang up. These were designed to democratize decision-making in factories, communes, schools, local governments, and residential neighbourhoods. Reflecting the experimental temper of these years, the Revolutionary Committees were widely varied in their composition and activities. However, a factory Revolutionary Committee might consist of roughly equal portions of workers, revolutionary cadres, and members of the Workers' Propaganda Team (an outside group of political activists, including PLA soldiers, who were sent to the various factories, communes, and neighbourhoods to help the people carry out their own Cultural Revolution). The factory workers on the Committee would represent every age and rank within the work force.

Everywhere, people debated incessantly, seeking to identify the enemy—the capitalist roaders and social revisionists among their own numbers. Sometimes open conflict broke out between various factions or between workers and invading Red Guards. At its height, the

Cultural Revolution seemed to plunge China into a chaotic, undisciplined mass orgy of political re-examination and recrimination.

In the term "Cultural Revolution," the Communist definition of "culture" included politics and political thought; but there was also a "proletarian revolution" in the field of culture as we know it. Mao's wife, Chiang Ch'ing, paid particular attention to the arts, and as a result of her activities during this period she rose from relative political obscurity to membership in the Politburo. Throughout the 1966–9 period, all artistic works came under detailed scrutiny for hidden non-revolutionary elements. Only a handful of new revolutionary operas, ballet productions, and films received official approval. At one stage, Mao's writings and the public press represented almost the whole body of acceptable literature in the Republic. All new artistic forms stressed the Cultural Revolution's message: commitment to socialist values, dedication to revolution, and self-reliance (collective, not individual).

From late 1968 on, it became evident that the Cultural Revolution was coming to an end. Schools gradually reopened and factory

Scene from The Red Detachment of Women, *one of the most famous of the new ballet productions during the Cultural Revolution.*

schedules resumed normal workdays, unpunctuated by "struggle sessions." Millions of Red Guard youth were ordered to the countryside, particularly to the sparsely populated interior border regions, to enable them to give concrete expression to their dedication to socialist values. The PLA, some of whom had recently acted on propaganda teams to stir up revolutionary activity at all levels of society, now acted firmly to restrain any effort by those who sought to continue the convulsions of recent years. By the summer of 1971, the host of revolutionary slogans, posters, and portraits of Mao, plastered over the façades of all public buildings, had disappeared, and were replaced by new injunctions calling for unity and hard work. Premier Chou En-lai, a prominent leader from the earliest days of the CCP, and one who was particularly noted for his administrative abilities, emerged as the prime force behind the reassertion of national order, while Chairman Mao remained the unchallenged ideological leader. Lin Piao, so recently hailed as Chairman Mao's second-in-command, abruptly disappeared from view, to be exposed after his death as a traitor. According to Chinese sources, he had died in an airplane crash in Mongolia while fleeing to Russia, having been discovered plotting to assassinate Mao.

The total preoccupation with domestic events in the late 1960s was followed, in the early seventies, by a new wave of diplomatic openness. France's recognition of the PRC and the exchange of ambassadors with Peking in 1964 marked almost the only significant alteration in Chinese diplomatic relations with western countries since the early fifties, although trade with the non-socialist world had steadily increased, particularly after the Sino-Soviet "split." In October 1970, Canada formally established diplomatic relations with Peking, followed shortly by Italy and Belgium. In the fall of 1971, the United Nations recognized the right of the PRC to represent the Chinese people. In February 1972, Richard M. Nixon, President of the United States, officially visited China, marking a fundamental shift in world politics. Subsequently a formula was worked out which dramatically reduced hostility between the two nations, although it did not go as far as establishing full diplomatic recognition. During 1972, West Germany, Japan, Australia, and New Zealand all recognized the PRC and

In order of importance, Communist leaders cast their ballots at the Ninth Party Congress in 1969. Mao is followed by Lin Piao and Chou En-lai. Third from the right is Mme Mao, Chiang Ch'ing, whose left-wing group fell from high positions after Mao's death in 1976.

exchanged diplomatic representatives, and Britain concluded a new agreement with Peking by which both raised their formal diplomatic representation to full ambassadorial level. Foreign visitors once again flocked to China, and exchanges of students and faculty were quietly arranged between China and several countries, including Australia, Britain, and Canada.

The Cultural Revolution was over, but its impact remained. How much it permanently influenced the Chinese people is a question for the future. One example of its continuing influence is the May Seventh Cadre Schools, which sprang up during those convulsive years. These were designed originally as re-education centres for those cadres identified during the Cultural Revolution as being guilty of undesirable tendencies in thought or behaviour. Set up throughout the country, these ''schools'' sought to correct erroneous ideas and rekindle revolutionary fervour by a combination of hard physical work and directed political study. Typically, the schools were located in rural areas, on land so poor, hilly, or dry as to discourage the local peasantry from any great use of it for productive purposes. Urban bureaucrats and teachers were sent to these centres in the countryside, which, in the Maoist perspective, was the source of purer revolutionary values. Here, as "students," they would fulfil the injunction to learn from the masses, and would apply the lessons initially in actual work on the land and later in their normal occupations. By 1972 the schools had lost most of their punitive character and had become an established feature of society. Specific schools were designated for short periods of attendance by all cadres on a rotational basis. By the mid-1970s they were looked upon almost as rural havens where urban bureaucrats and teachers could temporarily escape the pressures of their jobs, although such release was still acquired only by working with their hands as well as their minds, and still with the purpose of renewing their dedication to the principles of Maoist revolution.

One thing was clear to the foreign visitor to China after the Cultural Revolution. Out of the chaos and disruption of those years had come a new vitality. China had emerged strong and confident, and after years of comparative isolation it was becoming more actively a part of the world. This did not signal any lessening of revolutionary zeal. Chairman Mao had emphasized that the revolution remained a continuing process. The future would not be the same as the past or the present; new cultural upheavals—even new cultural revolutions—would again be required to change patterns of thought and to renew commitment to basic principles.

China in the Seventies

In late August 1973, the Tenth Party Congress met in Peking. Officially it met for only five days, and public announcement of its having taken place was made only after it closed on August 28. Very little is known of the details of this important event. Among its products, however, were the newly elected Central Committee and, very soon afterwards, the new Politburo. Both reflected the purge of Lin Piao and those associated with him, and there was a considerable drop in the number of military cadres active within these central decision-making bodies. Equally notable was the reappearance of several leadership figures who had suffered discredit and removal from official posts during the height of the Cultural Revolution.

Significantly, Premier Chou En-lai's report to the Congress officially confirmed earlier rumours concerning the circumstances of Lin Piao's disgrace. Chou described how Lin had attempted a coup d'état in mid-1970, and again in early September 1971. With the failure of the second attempt, which included a plan to assassinate Mao Tse-tung, Lin boarded a plane and fled in the direction of Russia, only to die in a crash in Outer Mongolia. Lin's intentions, and the new official perspective on his role in recent Chinese history, were summarized by Chou:

> Lin Piao and his handful of sworn followers were a counter-revolutionary conspiratorial clique "who never showed up without a copy of *Quotations* [i.e., the famous 'Little Red Book'] in hand and never opened their mouths without shouting 'Long Live [Chairman Mao]' and who spoke nice things to your face but stabbed you in the back." The essence of the counter-revolutionary revisionist line they pursued and the criminal aim of the counter-revolutionary armed coup d'état they launched were to usurp the supreme power of the Party and the state, thoroughly betray the line of the Ninth [Party] Congress, radically change the Party's basic line and policies for the entire historical period of socialism, turn the Marxist–Leninist Chinese Communist Party into a revisionist, fascist party, subvert the dictatorship of the proletariat and restore capitalism. Inside China, they wanted to reinstate the landlord and bourgeois classes, which our Party, Army and people had overthrown with their own hands under the leadership of Chairman Mao, and to institute a feudal-comprador-fascist dictatorship. Internationally, they wanted to capitulate to Soviet revisionist social-imperialism and ally themselves with imperialism, revisionism and reaction to oppose China, communism and revolution.[58]

Along with Chou's denunciation of Lin Piao, another report to the Congress signalled the rise of the thirty-six-year-old Wang Hung-wen to a place in the central leadership. A new Politburo member, Wang had played an important role in Shanghai during the Cultural Revolution, and was recognized as a new top-ranking member of the Party (after Mao Tse-tung and Chou En-lai). Wang's report was significant in that it touched on revisions of the 1969 Party Constitution passed by the Ninth Party Congress. Besides dropping all references to Lin Piao, the revised Constitution included a pronouncement on "the theory of continued revolution" (the italics are added):

The basic programme of the Communist Party of China is the complete overthrow of the bourgeoisie and all other exploiting classes, the establishment of the dictatorship of the proletariat in place of the dictatorship of the bourgeoisie and the triumph of socialism over capitalism. The ultimate aim of the Party is the realization of communism.

Through more than 50 years of arduous struggle, the Communist Party of China has led the Chinese people in winning complete victory in the new-democratic revolution, great victories in socialist revolution and socialist construction and great victories in the Great Proletarian Cultural Revolution.

Socialist society covers a considerably long historical period. Throughout this historical period, there are classes, class contradictions and class struggle, there is the struggle between the socialist road and the capitalist road, there is the danger of capitalist restoration and there is the threat of subversion and aggression by imperialism and [Russian] social-imperialism. *These contradictions can be resolved only by depending on the theory of continued revolution* under the dictatorship of the proletariat and on practice under its guidance.

Such is China's Great Proletarian Cultural Revolution, a great political revolution carried out under the conditions of socialism by the proletariat against the bourgeoisie and all other exploiting classes to consolidate the dictatorship of the proletariat and prevent capitalist restoration. *Revolutions like this will have to be carried out many times in the future.*[59]

Despite the reassertion of control that ended the Cultural Revolution, these words were a reaffirmation of the positive value of the dynamic revolutionary spirit of those years between 1966 and 1969.

In August 1973 (as the Tenth Party Congress was meeting), a philosopher at an important university in Canton criticized Confucius in an article in the *People's Daily*, China's largest national newspaper. Using the Marxist view of historical progress through certain stages (see page 161), he insisted that Confucius had represented a declining, slave-owning aristocracy, and that his entire thought structure had been a defence of that class's interests, which were being challenged by new "progressive" elements within seventh-century B.C.E. society. To underline the modern relevance of this seemingly academic argument, the author concluded that "Criticism of Confucius' reactionary thought is therefore helpful to taking part in actual class-struggle [of today]. . . ."[60]

Other writers took up this view of Confucius and expanded its implications by contrasting the "reactionary" character of Confucius' ideas with the "progressive" nature of Legalist thought. For centuries, Chinese thinkers had viewed Ch'in Shih Huang-ti, the first emperor of imperial China (see page 27), as the epitome of cruelty. In contrast, the new view of the 1970s praised him as a progressive ruler when considered within the proper historical context. They argued that his centralizing efforts (including the burning of the books and the persecution of dissenting intellectuals) were necessary steps to consolidate the new dictatorship of the feudal landlord class—the "progressives" of the seventh to the third centuries B.C.E., according to this theory —against the old slave-owning aristocrats championed by Confucius. As this view spread through the public press, it was clear that the argument over ancient history had serious contemporary implications. Chinese writers castigated those revisionists who vilified Ch'in Shih Huang-ti and supported "the Confuciuses of contemporary China such as Liu Shao-ch'i and Lin Piao." The mention of revisionists, and particularly the singling out of Liu and Lin, were nation-wide signals that this hitherto scholarly argument was developing into a new political campaign.

The campaign took on sharper focus with a 1974 New Year's Day editorial that appeared simultaneously in the *People's Daily* (the Party's ideological newspaper), and the *Liberation Army Daily* (the main PLA newspaper). In it, the writer linked the ancient Chinese philosopher, who had lived 2 500 years earlier, with the discredited CCP leader:

It is necessary in the first place to continue to do a good job of deepening the movement to criticize Lin Piao and rectify the style of work. Lin Piao's line was a revisionist line. . . . Criticism of Lin Piao, of the ultra-Rightist nature of his line, is criticism of revisionism. We should make full use of Lin Piao, a teacher by negative example, to educate the cadres and the masses on combating and preventing revisionism. . . . It is necessary to continue to criticize the ideas of worshipping Confucius and opposing the Legalist school, and in the course of the criticism build up the ranks of Marxist theorists. Both reactionaries at home and abroad and the ring-leaders of the opportunist lines worship Confucius. Therefore, criticizing

Confucius is a component part of the criticism of Lin Piao. We should continue to carry out the Party's policy of uniting, educating and remoulding the intellectuals. We hope that they (our intellectuals) will continue to make progress and that, in the course of work and study, they will gradually acquire the communist world outlook, get a better grasp of Marxism–Leninism and become integrated with the workers and peasants. We hope they will not stop halfway, or, what is worse, slip back, for there will be no future for them in going backwards.[61]

A month later, the *People's Daily* described this ideological debate as a mass campaign, called by Chairman Mao, to criticize Lin Piao and Confucius. Lin was castigated as a "bourgeois careerist, conspirator, double-dealer, renegade and traitor, an out-and-out disciple of Confucius who opposed the Legalist school, attacked Chin Shih Huang[-ti] and used the doctrines of Confucius and Mencius to seek to usurp Party leadership, seize state power and restore capitalism."[62]

Meetings and rallies were called throughout the country to carry out the "Criticize Confucius, Criticize Lin Piao" campaign. The debates ranged widely. Queries were made as to whether western classical music, as the product of the capitalist society of eighteenth- and nineteenth-century Europe, really had any place in the new socialist China. A film on China, made in 1972 by the Italian director Antonioni, came in for very sharp criticism, and new revolutionary operas were subjected to intense re-examination. Western observers watched for political implications. Some minor leaders did suffer as the result of being identified as local examples of Lin Piao's influence, but no national figures came in for open attack (though, at one time, speculation centred on the possibility that the ailing Chou En-lai was the ultimate target). There was a great stress on the training of worker-peasant-soldier theorists (i.e., a "mass intelligentsia"), which would be less élitist and more involved in physical labour than the old-style intellectual class. In the eyes of Mao and his followers, the traditional Confucian separation of society into those who worked with their minds and those who worked with their hands had continued to affect contemporary Chinese attitudes, and thus the remnants of past viewpoints became a prime target of this new ideological campaign.

The references to a new mass intelligentsia also indicated the broad social impact of this campaign to discredit both an ancient historical figure and a recent political leader. For the new intellectuals of the masses were to be proponents of new values in the long struggle of the Communists (and before them, the other Chinese modernists) to break the lingering hold of traditional social attitudes and practices on the mind of the average Chinese. The particular target of local campaigns was the residue of resistance to modern views on family relations, birth control, and female equality—a clinging, that is, to the complex network of relationships and values which centuries of Confucianism had ingrained in the everyday life of the Chinese people.

On October 1, 1974, the People's Republic celebrated its twenty-fifth anniversary. The editorial that appeared in all the main newspapers summed up the prevailing attitude toward the accomplishments and continuing problems of contemporary China:

> Earth-shaking changes have taken place in China in the past 25 years. Old China, poor and backward, has changed into socialist New China with the beginnings of prosperity. Under the guidance of Chairman Mao's proletarian revolutionary line and under the leadership of the Communist Party of China, we have in the main completed the socialist transformation of the ownership of the means of production and have carried out successive socialist revolutions, each time more deeply, on the political and ideological fronts. We have won big victories in the Great Proletarian Cultural Revolution in which the bourgeois headquarters of Liu Shao-ch'i (*sic*) and of Lin Piao have been smashed, Marxism–Leninism–Mao Tse-tung Thought has permeated people's thinking, socialist new things have bloomed everywhere, and the dictatorship of the proletariat has been further consolidated. As we persevere in the principle of maintaining independence and keeping the initiative in our own hands and relying on our own efforts, our socialist construction is briskly advancing and an independent and fairly complete system of industry and of national economy as a whole based on socialist agriculture is taking shape. Imperialist and social-imperialist [i.e., Russian] encirclement, blockade, aggression and subversion have all ended in ignominious defeat.[63]

The editorial called for a greater effort to carry out the mass criticism of Lin Piao and Confucius:

> By adhering to the principle of making the past serve the present and by applying the Marxist stand, viewpoint and method, we must criticize the

doctrines of Confucius and Mencius and sum up the historical experience of the struggle between the Confucian and Legalist schools and of class struggle as a whole in order to serve the current class struggle and the struggle to oppose and prevent revisionism and to help consolidate the dictatorship of the proletariat. Attention should also be paid to training Marxist theoretical workers and enlarging their ranks in the course of struggle. In the movement to criticize Lin Piao and Confucius, we must further heighten our consciousness of the struggle between the two lines, push forward struggle-criticism-transformation on all fronts and further strengthen our adherence to the socialist orientation.[64]

Thus the debate continued, with ancient philosophies and traditional social practices very much a part of the contemporary battle to create the new socialist society.

Finally, in late January 1975, the Fourth National People's Congress met in Peking and adopted a new Constitution for the People's Republic. Much shorter than its 1954 predecessor, this Constitution emphasized even more the Chinese preference for individuals, ideals, and programs, rather than rigid political structures and fine legalistic definitions. The office of Chairman of the Republic was abolished, and the armed forces were declared the responsibility of the Chairman of the Central Committee of the Chinese Communist Party. Furthermore, the revolutionary committees of the Cultural Revolution were made official local administrative bodies. With its great stress on "Serve the People" (one of the most common slogans in the China of the 1970s), this new Constitution was obviously a piece of Mass Line legislation. Extremely short (it contained only fifteen articles on "General Principles" and fifteen on "The Structure of the State"), it was written in very simple Chinese, putting the state's fundamental document within the grasp of the average citizen, without need for professional interpretation by either lawyers or politicians. It stood, therefore, as another example of the Chinese Communist effort to achieve a transition to modernity (in their terms) by involving everyone in the process.

The experiment to create a new China continues. A new era is obviously in the making with the passing away of many prominent figures in twentieth-century history. Chiang Kai-shek died in 1975. Many Communist leaders are now missing — 1976 saw the deaths of

Chou En-lai, the tireless administrator, and of Chu Teh, the eminent army figure. In September of 1976 came the passing of Mao Tse-tung, the most prominent of the generation of leaders who spanned the years of the early revolutionary struggles, the Long March and Yenan Years, and the post-1949 debates and experiments to define the future China.

In perspective, we can now see communism, with its modern thrust and original theoretical base in European civilization, as an integral part of the long and complex history of China. Whether or not we approve of the methods used in the new China, or agree on the practicality (or the desirability) of the goals, we cannot afford to be ignorant of the struggles—the triumphs and the failures—of the world's most populous nation. One of history's oldest and richest civilizations, China now proposes to "build socialism independently and with the initiative in our own hands, through self-reliance, hard struggle, diligence and thrift and by going all out, aiming high and achieving greater, faster, better and more economical results. . . ."[65] Its continuing experiences demand our knowledgeable attention.

Analysis

1. Was the period of the Great Proletarian Cultural Revolution a positive or a negative event in China's development? Why?
2. Discuss the advantages and disadvantages of the rotation system of mental and physical work. Could this be applied in our country? How?
3. Is the public discrediting of such figures as Confucius and Lin Piao a sign of health or decadence? Why?
4. Why did Mao support the ideal of on-going revolution? Can such an ideal be realized?

SECTION IV   SUMMARY AND RESEARCH

1. Confucianism and Marxism are compatible. Discuss.

2. What arguments could Marx and Lenin have used against Mao's view that the peasant is the key to revolution?

3. Three great figures emerged in China from 1911 to 1945: Sun Yat-sen, Chiang Kai-shek, and Mao Tse-tung. Sun failed from a lack of political will, Chiang from a lack of political vision, while Mao succeeded because he possessed both will and vision. Do you agree? Why? Why not?

4. Sidney Hook, in his book *The Hero in History*, defines the hero in history as the event-making man, in contrast to the eventful man: ''The event-making man, on the other hand, finds a fork in the historical road, but he also helps . . . to create it. . . . It is the hero as event-making man who leaves the positive imprint of his personality upon history—an imprint that is still observable after he has disappeared from the scene. The merely eventful man whose finger plugs a dike or fires the shot that starts a war is rarely aware of the nature of the alternative he faces and of the train of events his act sets off.'' According to Hook's definition, would any or all of the following qualify as hero? Why? (a) Sun Yat-sen, (b) Chiang Kai-shek, (c) Mao Tse-tung.

5. Draw a diagram which clearly shows the organization of the CCP during the Japanese occupation. Include *all* types of organization in your diagram. Why was this organization effective?

6. ''The course of Chinese history in the twentieth century reflects the continuous dual influences of the United States and Russia.'' Is this an accurate statement for the period 1900 to 1949? Which was more influential?

7. Compare the first decade of the Chinese revolution to the decade 1917 to 1927 in the Soviet Union. Explain the similarities and differences.

8. Compare the land reform by the Chinese in the 1950s with that of the U.S.S.R. in the 1930s. Account for the differences. How do you explain the relative success of the Chinese?

9. To what extent has the status of women been affected by the revolution since 1949?

FINAL SUMMARY AND RESEARCH

1. In his preface the author states that his "approach is generally sympathetic" to China. Do you think that the author's evaluation of his attitude is correct? Why?

2. The most striking characteristic of modern China is not its revolutionary break with the past but the continuance of the past in the revolution. Do you agree? Discuss.

3. Historically, China has been faced with the tension between centrifugal forces (forces of disunity) and centripetal forces (forces of unity). Is the Communist government dealing with this problem more effectively or less effectively than previous governments? Explain.

4. Has the Chinese experiment since 1949 been sufficiently dynamic and on-going to give those who did not participate before 1949 the feeling of being part of a revolutionary society? Explain your answer.

5. Assess the joint editorial of October 1, 1974, found on pages 221–2. To what extent do you think that the claims in this editorial are justified?

6. Make one list of the ways in which China has changed for the better since 1949 and one of the ways in which China has changed for the worse. What do your lists reveal about your own values?

Pronunciation Guide

Note: The following is only a rough approximation to enable those who know no Chinese to pronounce correctly the Chinese names mentioned in the text. Names are transliterated the first time they appear, and are in the order in which they appear. Words which sound as they appear are not included. (The nearest equivalent English sounds have been used, but note that for this guide, *ie* is pronounced as in t*ie*, *oo* as in lo*o*k, *ow* as in *ow*l, *u* as in gl*u*e.)

Chapter 1	
Yangtze	yong dzoo
Sikiang	shee jyong

Chapter 2	
Yenan	yee nan
Honan	hoo nan

Chapter 3	
Shang	shong
Chou	joe
Ch'in	chin
Sui	sway
T'ang	tong
Sung	soong
Yuan	ywon
Ch'ing	ching
Taiwan	tie won
Tao-kang	dow gwong
T'ien	tyan
Huang-ti	hwong dee
hsien	shee an
chin-shih	jin sheer
chu-jen	ju run
hsiu-ts'ai	sh-o tsie
fu	fu
sheng	shung

Chapter 4	
Tao	dow

Li Ssu	lee s-soo
Lao-tzu	low dzoo
Chuang-tzu	jwong dzoo
Ch'u	chu
Chu Hsi	ju shee
Lu	lu
Shantung	shan doong
Ju	ru
Tzu Lu	dzu lu
Fan Ch'ih	fan chr
yang	yong
Wei	way
ching	jing
Ch'an	chan

Chapter 6	
Chung-kuo	joong gwo
Han Yu	hon yu
Ch'ien-lung	chee-an loong

Chapter 7	
Canton	can ton
Lin Tse-hsu	lin dzoo shu
Liuchiu	lu chu
Taiwan	tie wan
Shanghai	shong hie
Liaotung	lee-ow doong
Tientsin	tyan sin
Tsungli yamen	dzoong-lee yah-men

Chapter 8

Taiping	tie ping
Nien	ny an
Hung Hsiu-ch'uan	hoong shu chwan
T'ung-chih	toong jer
Li Hung-chang	lee hoong jong
Tz'u-hsi	dzu shee
Hsien-feng	shee-an foong

Chapter 9

Chang Chih-tung	jong jer doong
T'an Ssu-t'ung	tan s-soo toong
Hu Han-min	hu han min
Sun Yat-sen	sun yat sen
Kuomintang	gwo min dong
Meiji	may jee
Itō	ee toe
Tsingtao	tsing dow
Yen Fu	yen fu
Foochow	fu joe
Peiyang	bay yong
K'ang Yu-wei	kong yo way
Liang Ch'i-ch'ao	lee-ang chee chow
Chihli	jer lee
I-ho ch'üan	ee hoo jwan

Chapter 10

San Min Chu I	san min ju ee
Wuchang	wu chong
Yuan Shih-k'ai	yu-an sher kie
Whampoa	wam po ah
Chiang Kai-shek	jyong kie shek
Chou En-lai	joe en lie
Lin Piao	lin b-yow

pai-hua	bie hwah
ku-wen	gu wen

Chapter 11

Chekiang	jeh jyong
Paoting	bow ding
Soong Mei-ling	soong may ling
Shensi	shen shee
Manchukuo	man chu gwo
Chang Tso-lin	jong dzo lin
Chang Hsueh-liang	jong sweh lee-ang
P'u-i	pu ee
Sian	see an
Chungking	choong king
Hwai	h-wie
Peiping	bay ping

Chapter 13

Ch'en Tu-hsiu	chun du sho
Li Ta-chao	lee dah jow
Mao Tse-tung	mow dzoo doong
Ching-kang-shan	jing gong shan
Hunan	hu nan
Kiangsi	jyong shee
Chu Teh	ju deh

Chapter 15

Liu Shao-ch'i	lee-o show chee
hsia-fang	shee-ah fang

Chapter 16

Chiang Ch'ing	jyong ching
Wang Hung-wen	wong hoong wen

Sources

1. T. H. White and A. Jacoby, *Thunder out of China* (New York: Wm. Sloane Associates, Inc., 1946), 22–3.
2. Dun J. Li, ed., *The Essence of Chinese Civilization* (Princeton, N.J.: D. Van Nostrand Co., 1967), 257.
3. White and Jacoby, *Thunder out of China*, 170–1.
4. R. Latham, trans., *The Travels of Marco Polo* (London: Penguin Books, 1958), 195.
5. L. J. Callagher, S.J., trans., *China in the Sixteenth Century: The Journals of Matthew Ricci, 1583–1610* (New York: Random House, 1953), 36–7.
6. Li, *The Essence of Chinese Civilization*, 30.
7. Wm. T. deBary, *et al.*, comp., *Sources of Chinese Tradition* (New York: Columbia University Press, 1960), I, 51.
8. *Ibid.*, 59.
9. *Ibid.*, 77.
10. *Ibid.*, 93.
11. *Ibid.*, 96.
12. *Ibid.*, 29–30.
13. Li, *The Essence of Chinese Civilization*, 74–5.
14. *Mencius*, trans. by D. C. Lau (Penguin Books Ltd., 1970), 103.
15. deBary, *Sources of Chinese Tradition*, I, 373.
16. S. Y. Teng and J. K. Fairbank, eds., *China's Response to the West* (Cambridge, Mass.: Harvard University Press, 1961), 19.
17. R. Dawson, *The Chinese Chameleon* (London: Oxford University Press, 1967), 55.
18. Quoted in A. Reichwein, *China and Europe: Intellectual and Artistic Contacts in the Eighteenth Century* (London: Kegan Paul, 1925), 89.
19. Quoted in S. C. Miller, *The Unwelcome Immigrant* (Berkeley and Los Angeles: University of California Press, 1969), 16.

20. *Punch*, April 10, 1858, as quoted in Dawson, *The Chinese Chameleon*, 133.

21. Wm. C. Hunter, *Bits of Old China* (London: Kegan Paul, Trench & Co., 1855; reprint, Taipei: Ch'eng-wen Publishing Co., 1966), 38–9.

22. Wm. C. Hunter, *The "Fan Kwae" at Canton before Treaty Days: 1825–1844* (London: Kegan Paul, Trench & Co., 1882; reprint, Taipei: Ch'eng-wen Publishing Co., 1965), 155.

23. Quoted in J. K. Fairbank, *Trade and Diplomacy on the China Coast, 1842–1854* (Cambridge, Mass.: Harvard University Press, 1953), 83.

24. L.W. Pye, *China: An Introduction* (Boston: Little, Brown & Co., 1972), 112.

25. Teng and Fairbank, *China's Response to the West*, for Chang Chih-tung, 169; for T'an Ssu-t'ung, 160; for Boxers, 190. For Hu Han-min, see deBary, *Sources of Chinese Tradition*, II, 101.

26. Quoted in Paul A. Cohen, *China and Christianity: The Missionary Movement and the Growth of Chinese Antiforeignism, 1860–1870* (Cambridge, Mass.: Harvard University Press, 1963), 85, as in his "Ch'ing China: Confrontation with the West, 1850–1900," in J. B. Crowley, ed., *Modern East Asia: Essays in Interpretation* (New York: Harcourt, Brace & World, 1970), 53.

27. "The Manifesto of the T'ung-meng-hui, 1905," in Teng and Fairbank, *China's Response to the West*, 228.

28. Dr. R.B. McClure, Oral History Project: "Canadians in East Asia," Session I, October 30, 1970; transcript (York University, 1970), 15–17.

29. John A. Harrison, *China Since 1800* (New York: Harcourt, Brace & World, Inc., 1967), 160.

30. White and Jacoby, *Thunder out of China*, 275.

31. Joseph W. Stilwell, *The Stilwell Papers*, arranged and edited by T. H. White (New York: MacFadden-Bartell Corp., 1962), 100.

32. *Ibid.*, 157.

33. *Ibid.*, 251.

34. Sun Yat-sen, *San Min Chu I: The Three Principles of the People*, trans. by F. W. Price (Shanghai, 1927), 5.

35. *Ibid.*, 114–15.

36. Quoted in O. E. Clubb, *Twentieth Century China* (New York: Columbia University Press, 1964), 283.

37. John F. Melby, *The Mandate of Heaven: Record of a Civil War, China 1945–49* (Toronto: University of Toronto Press, 1968), 239–41.

38. Douglas S. Paauw, "The Kuomintang and Economic Stagnation, 1928–38," in A. Feuerwerker, ed., *Modern China* (Englewood Cliffs, N.J.: Prentice-Hall, 1964), 130.

39. Margo S. Gewurtz, "Tsou T'ao-fen: The Sheng-huo Years, 1925–1933," Ph.D. thesis (Cornell University, 1972), 84.

40. Harrison, *China Since 1800*, 191.

41. "Report on an Investigation of the Peasant Movement in Hunan," in C. Brandt, B. Schwartz, and J. K. Fairbank, *A Documentary History of Chinese Communism* (New York: Atheneum, 1973), 80.

42. J. Ch'en, ed., *Mao* (Englewood Cliffs, N.J.: Prentice-Hall, 1969), 87.

43. J. Ch'en, *Mao and the Chinese Revolution* (London: Oxford University Press, 1965), 189.

44. *Ibid.*, 200.

45. Paraphrased from *ibid.*, 254.

46. Opening Speech at People's Political Consultative Conference, as reported in *People's Daily*, September 22, 1949.

47. "On New Democracy," January 19, 1940, quoted in deBary, *Sources of Chinese Tradition*, II, 224.

48. "Common Programme of the People's Political Consultative Conference," Article 15, in Otto B. Van der Sprenkel, *New China: Three Views* (London: Turnstile Press, 1950), 204–5.

49. "On the People's Democratic Dictatorship," in Brandt, Schwartz, and Fairbank, *A Documentary History of Chinese Communism*, 456.

50. Peter S. H. Tang, *Communist China Today*, vol. II, *Chronology and Documentary Supplement* (New York: Frederick A. Praeger, 1958), 91–2.

51. Franklin W. Houn, *A Short History of Chinese Communism* (Englewood Cliffs, N.J.: Prentice-Hall, 1967), 138–40.

52. *Ibid.*, 88.

53. "Get Organized," in Ch'en, *Mao*, 90.

54. See K. Gupta, "How Did the Korean War Begin?", *The China Quarterly*, 52 (October/December, 1972), 699–716; and following discussion, *ibid.*, 54 (April/June, 1973).

55. B. Frolic, "Research Notes on Visit to P.R.C., June 1971," unpublished manuscript, 11–23.

56. "On New Democracy," in Ch'en, *Mao*, 98–9.

57. *Ibid.*, 99–101.

58. *China Quarterly*, 56 (October/December 1973), 807–8. (The quotation within Chou's speech was probably from a denunciation of Lin that was well known to his Chinese audience.)

59. *Ibid.*, 820.

60. *Peking Review*, No. 41 (October 12, 1973), as in *China Quarterly*, 57 (January/March 1974), 208.

61. *Peking Review*, No. 1 (January 1, 1973), as in *China Quarterly*, 58 (April/June 1974), 406.

62. *China Quarterly*, 58 (April/June 1974), 407.

63. *China Quarterly*, 61 (March 1975), 177.

64. *Ibid.*, 178.

65. Preamble to *The Constitution of the People's Republic of China* (Peking: Foreign Language Press, 1975), 8–9.

INDEX

This short index is selective, containing key names and topics, and themes in which students might find project interest.

77 87 97 08 18 28 38 48 58   AP   9 8 7 6 5 4 3 2 1